PLAIN TALK

Corey Washington (M. Ed)

PLAIN TALK

Digging a Little Deeper

Volume 2

Copyright © 2010 by Corey Washington (M. Ed).

Library of Congress Control Number:		2010906643
ISBN:	Hardcover	978-1-4500-9426-9
	Softcover	978-1-4500-9425-2
	Ebook	978-1-4500-9427-6

All rights reserved. No part of this book may be reproduced or transmitted in any form or by any means, electronic or mechanical, including photocopying, recording, or by any information storage and retrieval system, without permission in writing from the copyright owner.

This book was printed in the United States of America.

To order additional copies of this book, contact:
Xlibris Corporation
1-888-795-4274
www.Xlibris.com
Orders@Xlibris.com
80715

Contents

CHAPTER ONE

Personal Tidbits

This chapter is a series of personal blogs, conflicts, and encounters as a result of my quest to engage people on Race.

Why did I Start the Plain Talk Series?

This is a question that I get asked all the time. I never really had aspirations of becoming a writer. When I was in school, we were always required to do a lot of writing. I always flourished when I was able to pick a topic that greatly interested me. When it came to topics that were picked for me, I frequently became uninspired in my writing. So when certain events happened in the summer of 2009, I became inspired to be a writer.

There were a series of three pivotal events that all happened around the same time that heavily influenced my decision to start the Plain Talk series:

1) **an article in a magazine on discrimination and racism**
2) **a special on CNN called "Black in America 2"**
3) **the Henry Louis Gates Jr. and Ofc. Crowley incident in Cambridge, Massachusetts**

Another interesting side point was a week or two before I became inspired a friend of mine, Franklin Mars, planted a subliminal seed. While we were fishing on a boat in North Augusta, South Carolina, he said I should write a book. He didn't say about race or any related topic that I actually did write about, but the idea of writing a book right then just didn't move me.

I must admit, I may have been suckered in somewhat by the media. After Skip Gates was involved in being arrested in his own home, the media began to call for a fresh dialogue on race. There were segments of the media calling the whole episode a **"teachable moment"**. Then Pres. Obama became involved by criticizing the Cambridge Police Department by saying they acted "stupidity". Finally, to smooth things over, Pres. Obama invited Skip Gates and Ofc. Crowley to the White House for the famous or infamous "Beer Summit". In the footage released thereafter, nobody, except for maybe Pres. Obama and VP Joe Biden, seemed to really be enjoying themselves. After the meeting, a small press conference was held, which seemed to suggest that the two parties (Gates/Crowley) just agreed to disagree. This is just pure speculation on my part, but it also seems that a gentleman's agreement was made to not talk about the incident anymore. "At least until the next big incident flares up".

What happened at the Beer Summit?
Did this "teachable moment" escape us?

It was too late as far as I was concerned, I had already formulated many ideas for a book discussing race in a manner that would be honest, evenhanded, and responsible. This book that I had in my head would not rely on statistics or theories. I wanted to write a book that would be personal and conversational. This book would educate the uninformed as well as remind and refresh the memory of those who are already knowledgeable about these subjects. Then, I wanted to provide practical examples for you to use in your everyday life. To help you out, I decided to put a reference section for slurs and stereotypes in the first volume. For example, when I list the various slurs and stereotypes for a wide variety of races, I followed that up with polarizing racial events so that you can see the extensive damage of relying on stereotypes to guide your views. Or, you can see the detrimental aftermath of slurs when considering famous incidents and famous people who have gotten into big trouble by using slurs. I had no idea concerning the onslaught of racial material that I would be bombarded with, ever since writing Plain Talk Volume One.

My desire for writing the Plain Talk series was also heightened by seeing the same pundits and so-called race experts on TV. I began to wonder: What makes these people more qualified to talk about race than me or the average intelligent person? We all have our own experiences on racism. We only know what others experience about racism, because they tell us. Also, I distinctly remember a conversation that I had with my friend Carlton Holden. We were discussing racism and stereotypes and our various experiences with situations involving race. Bear in mind that this conversation was about seven years before I wrote Plain Talk. Carlton was telling me about how he would experience unprovoked episodes of racism in Germany. He told me about how he was once called a Field Black (Feld Negar) or Field Nigger in Germany. Carlton also gave an example of a time that he was in Woolworth's in Germany. An elderly white lady in the store told him to get something off the shelf for her, but it was her extremely condescending attitude that made Carlton feel less than human. Carlton also talked about the violent exploits of skinheads in Germany. In one instance a skinhead called Carlton an African. Then he suggested that Carlton had better run.

At some point in our conversation, we began to play a sort of "call and response" stereotype game. One of us would call out a race, and then the other one would respond with as many stereotypes of that race as we could. The other person would fill in any stereotypes that the other person left out. After we finished, we were amazed at how many stereotypes we knew and agreed upon. Many of the stereotypes seemed comical when you think of the absurdity of all races doing one single thing. However, when stereotypes are used to denigrate, discriminate, or as an excuse to perpetrate many acts of crime or violence against certain races of people, then stereotypes are no laughing matter!

The most controversial part of Plain Talk Volume One is the use of slurs in the opening pages. Some may feel that using these slurs in my book opens the door for others with ulterior motives to be flippant or wonton in their use of slurs. Some may feel that the gratuitous use of slurs only gives ammunition to racists and other culturally immature people. That's only one train of thought. Do you really believe that people will not use slurs if they did not see them in a book? Highly unlikely!! If you carefully look at the treatment that I give slurs in Plain Talk, you will see that I don't encourage the use of them. I show the negative impact on society of these words.

If you pick up Plain Talk and you only read the part on slurs and stereotypes, then I have failed you as a writer. This book was designed in part to be a racial self-help book. Many views and attitudes that you may have brought with you when you first read Plain Talk are not supposed to remain with you after you have finished reading Plain Talk. It is just like the example that parents use about the subject of sex. Your kids can go online or talk to their friends about sex, or they can talk to their parents and other well-meaning responsible adults about sex. As a parent, which one would you choose? One thing's for sure, if you don't talk to your kids about sex, then they will get the information from somewhere else. The same thing goes with racism, stereotypes, and other issues related to race. People can go to the Internet and find racist jokes, false information about races (not presented as stereotypes, but presented as truthful information), or information that is designed for laughs rather than education. You can go on the Internet and find most of the definitions of slurs and discussions about stereotypes, but the presentation is not handled in a serious way.

People can go that route, or they can get the information from the Plain Talk series, where I present the information in a way that it deserves to be handled. We all know kids are very impressionable. If you don't teach them from an early age not to rely on stereotypes or use slurs, then they will just conform to the ideas of many of their peers around them. Who wants to subject their children to that way of thinking? On a more personal note, I caught my son Jordan using one of the slurs that I talk about in Plain Talk. He used the slur "Wigger" to refer to a teacher at his school. He picked this language up from some kids that he went to school with. I was quick to correct him and to tell him that not only did I not want him using the word, but I explained to him the hurtfulness of such a word. It is a constant battle to try to teach my son that you can't just repeat words or ideas said by other people. I constantly hear him parroting stereotypes that he has heard from other people. Parents, I know that it is not an easy job to raise children, but please continue to correct kids when it comes to racism, stereotypes, and slurs.

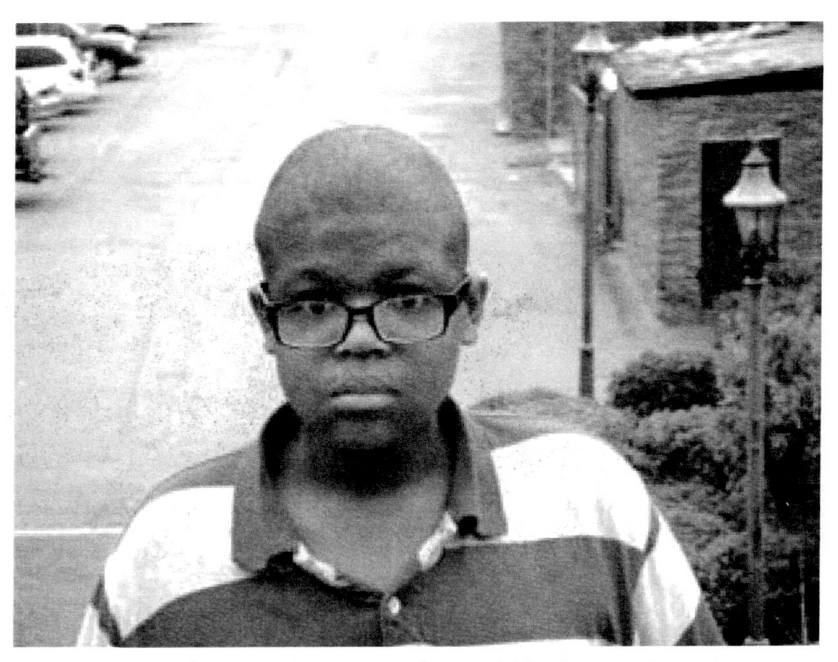

Parents, please continue to teach your kids about racism, slurs and stereotypes. It's tough counteracting the info and influences your child receives at school, but the end result is worth it.

Collection of Blogs related to Race

Since writing Plain Talk Vol. 1, I have written many blogs for various websites. (Benhasan.com, examiner.com, opposingviews.com, etc.) Here is a collection of all the ones pertaining to the subject at hand-Race.

A Day to Remember-African-Americans in the Augusta Media

Photo courtesy of Katonjua Johnson

Feb. 25th was a historic day for Tutt middle school and the CSRA. Media talent from WJBF, WFXG, WAGT, WRDW, Augusta Chronicle, Metro Courier, Comcast, and local radio were in attendance. Students and all invited guests were mesmerized by the energetic speeches and antics of all speakers. The program did not focus on one speaker, instead everyone was given an opportunity to speak. No matter who was speaking, the message was the same: Don't let anyone take your dreams away!

Fraendy Clervaud from WJBF got us started with a riveting and motivating speech. Then Jay Jefferies, WAGT forecaster, kept the momentum flowing with his effervescent personality. (I didn't know that Jay was classmates with Arsenio Hall and Steve Harvey.) Then the focus was on the print media, with representatives from the Augusta Chronicle, (Patricia

Burton) and Metro Courier (Ken J. Makin). Next, we were treated to the wonderful Helen Blocker Adams and Ben Hasan. Both of these talents are known in all circles as being two of Augusta's best community activists. Helen has her own talk radio show, The Helen Blocker Adams Show, on SonShine 103.7 FM/1600 AM WKZK, and Ben is the host of Comcast's Community Concerns. We finished up the speakers with the most represented station WRDW. Blayne Alexander, Matt Barnes, Ryan Calhoun, and Ashley Jeffery were all in attendance. Melissa Tune and Chris Thomas were also there and said a few words to the crowd.

In addition to the media speakers, the crowd was treated by the talented students and staff of Tutt middle school. The chorus and jazz band chose selections from the Jazz world. The highlight of the night may have belonged to the last performance of the program. Michael Bell, Carl Miller, and Kyle Scheel put on a wonderful display of break dancing that energized the crowd. Even Jay Jefferies couldn't resist the temptation to get up and dance. The crowd also went wild when Carl Miller gave a tribute to Michael Jackson, by dancing to Billie Jean. (Always a crowd pleaser!)

After the program, the participants from the media gathered for a group photo to commemorate the event. How else would anyone believe that we got that much talent in one room!! Hats off to the CSRA; we should all be proud of our African-Americans in our local media.

P.S.-For those who stuck around, we were treated to an impromptu jam session with Jay Jefferies on the drums. Jay was jamming to the Cream's Sunshine of your Love while one of Tutt's Bass players provided the backbone.

Is the Ku Klux Klan trying to make a comeback? (In the Deep South)

Shall the Klan rise again???

On Feb. 20th, everyone was focused on the small south Georgia town of Nahunta, as 500 people gathered for a Klan rally. I remember thinking to myself, this would never happen in Augusta, GA. People tend to have a certain stigma attached to small rural south Georgia towns. (remember the hanging effigy of Obama in Plains, GA.) It seems that I spoke too soon. The Aiken county S.C. area know as the "Valley" may have a Klan rally coming to the Burnettown-Clearwater community. The Klan is trying to soften it's stance among the populace by saying it wants to focus on immigration.

Please don't be fooled!! Don't think for a moment that they have stopped hating minorities and Catholics, and Jews. Don't believe the words of S.C. Klan leader Tim Bradly who says that people just misinterpret the Klan. If one were to venture to this proposed Klan rally, I'm sure they will hear the same old tired rhetoric from the past about how we need to keep America white. You will probably hear chants of White Power and maybe a few sprinkled N-words hear and there. After all, what's a Klan rally without a few sprinklings of the N-word.

The timing of this KKK rally is really suspect. It is scheduled for Saturday, April 3rd, which is the weekend before the Masters Tournament. There will be guests from all over the world. When they turn on the news, will they see great golfers, or a Klan rally? Another aspect to think about is the bringing in of other Klan members from other areas. I am sure that the Klan wants to make an impact on a national stage in order to get back into the limelight. Will the media oblige them? Let's hope the Augusta Chronicle doesn't give the Klan the same coverage that they gave that other charlatan Don "Moose" Lewis. If so, then it will be a disastrous April 3rd.

Tim Bradly is trying to change the image of the KKK.

The Augusta Chronicle-more harm than good?

Fair and unbalanced—You decide!! (Can't have it both ways.)

Does the Augusta Chronicle have an agenda at odds with the unification of Augusta? I have my doubts at times about their commitment to journalistic integrity!!!

Many of us know of a similar catch phrase from the Fox News Channel. That's what comes to mind when I think about the Augusta Chronicle. Many African-Americans in the community have taken issue with the far right agenda of the editorial board and the owner of the Chronicle, William "Billy" Morris. Some have even called for a boycott of the Augusta Chronicle. I am not going that far, but I just want people to think about the role of the media and how it relates to the perception of the community, as it pertains to education. In the book-Plain Talk Volume 1, It talks about the role of the media as it relates to race relations. In this particular situation, it's not race relations, but rather community relations that is a concern.

The whole incident starts, when I found out that the Augusta Chronicle and Preston Sparks ran a story about Tutt Middle School and an alleged Hit

List. The story was extremely late and did not correspond to the time of the actual event. No Hit List was ever found, which was evident from the very beginning. **Full Disclosure:** I have first hand knowledge of this event and to see the story in the daily newspaper was an eye opener.

Was the Chronicle trying to make Tutt look bad? Who was the original source of this story?

The story ran on Feb. 25th, the same day as Tutt's Black History Program honoring African-Americans in the local media. This historic assembly was featured on all the local T.V. stations in the Augusta area. It was great to see so many motivational speakers and personalities in one area. The story ran at least 6-7 times within a two day period on the local news. Yet, the Augusta Chronicle did not run one story on this momentous occasion. Even though they had representatives at the program, they refused to mention the black history program. Even Patrick Riley, a Communications major from Augusta State Univ. saw the importance of covering the event for the school newspaper, The Bell Ringer. So it's hard for me to believe that the Chronicle deemed the story not worthy of reporting.

The Chronicle has a history of running with outlandish news stories to try to sell papers. The most recent example was the ridiculous all-white basketball league proposed by Don "Moose" Lewis. This charlatan came out of nowhere with a shaky story on MLK day trying to make a name for himself. The Augusta Chronicle was the first to break this story and received world-wide attention for doing so. Their newspaper was quoted all over the world. This was a win-win for the Chronicle and Don Lewis, at the expense of everyone else. Now Don Moose Lewis is promoting boxing events in Nigeria. **He admitted to Creative Loafing that it was a publicity stunt.**

The real reason for writing this article is to implore the Augusta Chronicle to use better judgment when running stories. They have a huge bully pulpit, since Augusta doesn't have another daily paper. Their stories have a huge impact on the community as a whole. When you run stories about schools, people tend to hold on to the negatives. Let's at least make sure that there is a story to report. Furthermore, let's have some balance in the reporting of educational stories. Look for the good as well. Don't try grasping for straws when it comes to reporting the news, especially concerning children of our community. Please Augusta Chronicle and Preston Sparks, do more good to the community than harm.

John Mayer—He may not be getting a hood pass, but he is getting a free pass from the mainstream media.

When racial gaffes happen to famous people, I think we should all learn from them. You would think that people would have already learned from past celebrities that saying the N-word for a white celebrity is a toxic situation. It's a no win scenario. I have never heard a white person be able to successfully articulate their point by saying the N-word. Personally, I don't think any race of people should be saying the N-word. It is one of those words that has so much power because of the history behind it. It is unfortunate that some black people have lulled their white friends into a false sense of security by using the N-word around them. Some white people have become so comfortable that they have started to use the word as well. We know the mere use of a word does not make a person racist, but if you don't want to give off that impression, then don't use the N-word.

What disturbs me more than John Mayer's use of the N-word is his utter lack of respect for women and black people. He was so flippant in his speech, that he compared his penis to a former Grand Wizard of the KKK David Duke. There is nothing funny about the KKK. He used the word "aversion" to refer to his lack of attraction to black women. Aversion is a very strong word. There is nothing wrong with having a particular preference when it comes to women, but you don't have to put other races down in your assessment. He said he had a Benetton heart, but Benetton has been accused by some indigenous people in South America of being insensitive to their claim of land. So John Mayer's word selection was bad across the board.

Then, John Mayer showed a total disregard for the feelings of the past women in his life. His whole angle was one of the sexual objectification of women. He came off as extremely arrogant and self-centered. It is one thing to kiss and tell, but he threw Jessica Simpson totally under the bus. John must not realize that people have families that have to read this junk in the newspapers and on-line. So John not only gave a racist interview, but a sexist one as well.

When I said we should learn from the mistakes of celebrities, maybe I misspoke, because all of the mistakes that John Mayer made, we already knew. One lesson that I am learning has to do with the media's uneven treatment of celebrity gaffes. I am completely surprised that this story is not getting more play than the Kanye West /Taylor Swift story. The Kanye incident was light compared to the rudeness of John Mayer. The President of the United States and former President Jimmy Carter got involved with the Kanye West incident. In my book Plain Talk Volume 1, I talk about how the Media is selective in their being overly negative and critical of certain celebrities of color. I call this Media Theory: Piling it on. Since Kanye did not get a pass, nether should John Mayer get one. Sometimes you have to hold someone's feet to the fire for extended periods of time so that they will completely get the message. The coverage of this incident has been non-existent by the main stream media. That was the coverage that I was expecting for the Kanye West incident. Boy was I wrong.

The Piling it on Theory—Why Kanye and not John Mayer???

When some people do things they are just dead wrong. Their actions can not be defended. However, when African-Americans commit an egregious act, many Whites may wonder why the Black community rallies to their defense. It is not that the Black community condones or approves of these actions, but rather it has to do with the modern day phenomenon called: Piling it on. To put this theory to the test look at the Kanye West ordeal and the John Mayer Fiasco.

At the 2009 MTV Video Music Awards Kanye West rudely interrupted Taylor Swift's acceptance speech for Best Female Video. Kanye rushed the stage and politely, but inappropriately pointed out that he felt Beyonce should have won the award. He was booed and then left the stage. Normally people would talk about this incident the next day, but it wouldn't be a major news story on all the networks. I even heard one person say that Kanye assaulted Taylor Swift. Kanye seemed to feel remorse and apologized to Taylor Swift and her mother. This was not enough for some people, they wanted to "pile it on". Jay Leno even brought Kanye's dead mother into the fray in order to make him feel bad. As if that wasn't enough, the media baited President Obama into commenting on the situation. President Obama called Kanye West a "Jackass", in what he thought was an off-the-record conversation. Little did he know that his words were being taped. Even former President Jimmy Carter commented on the situation. Soon the media was asking every prominent person what they thought of Kanye West. I am not condoning the actions of Kanye West. He was wrong, but the coverage in the media was extremely excessive and negative.

Thus far, I did not mention the race of the person that Kanye offended. Since Taylor Swift is not Black, it may have seemed to many African-Americans that race was the reason that the media "piled it on". I hope that is not the case, but history says otherwise. When black people commit crimes or acts against one another, it is rarely covered in a sensational way. When an African-American does something against a non-African-American, then the media coverage becomes extremely sensationalized. It's not something that is obvious at the beginning, but as things drag on and you are able to look back and reflect, you can see the disparity in the treatment by the media.

When you compare the coverage of the Kanye West incident with the John Mayer incident, which one received the "Piling it on" treatment? It has to be Kanye's gaffe. John Mayer's situation barely made a blip on the Mainstream media's radar screen. Can you really say with a straight face that Kanye's actions were more offensive than John Mayer's? No!! So the question that I have is why the discrepancy? Is John Mayer being protected? Or is my "Piling it on" theory correct?

Here is an excerpt from Plain Talk Volume 1, where I give some solutions to the "Piling it on" theory:

> *What are the solutions to the "Piling it on" modern day phenomenon? Hopefully this book will open up a dialogue in order to explore solutions. That is my hope for many of the things discussed in this book. I hope people can discuss racial stereotypes/ slurs and how it erodes cooperation between the races and breeds distrust. I hope people can learn from the racial miscues of famous people and not make the same mistakes. I hope people will examine how the media influences the way we feel towards other races. Talk to people of all races and don't rely on the media to shape your views on other races. Let's look at polarizing racial events and see how our views on these events are shaped by stereotypes and life experiences. I hope people will see through the methods of racists and see that they are not that creative. They attempt to boost themselves up by childishly tearing other races down. Above all, if you learn nothing new from this book, I just want you to examine yourself and see if there is any room for improvement. And remember, there are more of us (non-racists) then there are of them. (racists)*

Comparing Apples to Oranges-Big Ben to Mike Vick, does the comparison fit?

With the history of racism and discrimination in the U.S., black people have become very observant. These skills have become very honed and polished over the years due to inequalities in all aspects of life. This is a trait that has led to many a court case being brought to flush out racism, to the benefit of generations to come. Some people have tried to underestimate these observational skills by marginalizing them. This has spawned the phrase "playing the race card".

When black people point out inequalities in non-essential aspects of life, is that really playing the race card? Not exactly. Equality should be upheld in important things as well as things that may seem trivial. When we talk about equality in the classroom for all races, we also want equality when it comes to portrayal in the media. Equality in the workforce should also translate into equality in the world of high school sports. It may seem like we are comparing apples to oranges, but that is not the case. You see, equality has a climate attached to it. When you taste equality in one area of your life, you want that same equality in other mundane areas of your life, especially when it is fair.

I recognize that there are more important examples of unfair treatment in the world, but I want to highlight a current case in the media to show how many black people become jaded. In my book Plain Talk Volume 1, I talk about how the media often sensationalizes the mishaps of celebrities of color. I used Michael Jackson, Kanye West, and Serena Williams as examples. I even had an article questioning why the Kanye West/Taylor Swift debacle was overblown in the media, as opposed to the John Mayer incident. If race is not an issue in these cases, it always comes off that way.

That brings me to another situation: the Ben Roethlisberger alleged sexual assault in Georgia. Many people of color are monitoring this situation internally to see if Big Ben will be treated the same way that Kobe Bryant or Michael Vick have been treated. So far he has been treated better. There have not been immediate calls for him to be released from his contract. He is still being treated by the media with kid gloves. I can remember when Kobe Bryant was accused of sexual assault, there was gratuitous coverage on all the cable news shows. Many people were already convicting him of rape. They were talking about Kobe registering as a sex offender in Colorado and what that would do to his life. His personal life was like an open book at that point.

Michael Vick was given the harshest treatment of any current athlete that I have ever seen. At first, he was already convicted of his crime before he went to trial in the court of the media. Once again, an overabundance of Mike Vick dog-fighting stories graced the news. It was lopsided as far as race when it came to Vick supporters and detractors. Even after being convicted and serving time in Kansas, many people were still showing hostility towards Mike Vick. To this day, I still read blogs where people are calling Mike Vick a dog murder and other vile names. If Big Ben is found guilty of sexual assault, will they have the same animosity towards him? I don't condone dog fighting or any type of violence towards animals, but does it equate with sexually violating another human being? Are we comparing apples to oranges? I don't want the media to treat Ben Roethlisberger with the same venom that they did Kobe and Vick. My point is, why did the media treat Kobe and Vick the way they did? Am I playing the race card for asking these questions? Am I comparing apples to oranges? You decide!!!

How would you feel?? Has celebrity worship gone too far??

Has the veneration of celebrities clouded society's judgment?

This is an update from the Big Ben Story. I first took the angle of why the media was giving preferential treatment to Big Ben. I thought maybe race had something to do with it. It turns out, that maybe the cops in Georgia may have been star struck. How would you feel if you were bringing charges against someone and you looked in the paper and saw them taking chummy pictures with the police. Actually, the same investigator who took your complaint is seen huddled up with Big Ben in a classic celebrity-celebrity fan style photo. It did not help that this same cop filed a sparse police report that did not initially name Big Ben as the culprit. The police chief of the Milledgeville PD came out with the company line that he was not bothered by these photos. You have uniformed police mixed with off-duty police taking photos with a man who hours later would be accused of sexual assault. How would you feel!!??

I can't imagine how a woman would feel knowing that the Good ole' boy system may be ready to protect the status quo. It's no wonder that women have a hard time reporting these incidents to police, whom many see as gatekeepers rather than protectors. Granted, this is a bad example that shines a bad light on the cops, but instead of protecting their own, cops should speak up and say: This is not protocol! When discrepancies happen among police, there is a tendency to remain silent out of respect to the officer. This leads to bad PR for the cops. It is almost akin to the dreaded street code of "Don't Snitch", common among criminals, rappers, and unfortunately our youth. I am mature enough to know that not all cops operate like this, but it sure does look bad. And if Big Ben is found not guilty, it cast a suspicious light on the whole affair. If there is a trial, it may have to be moved. Don't worry, I won't suggest Augusta as an alternate location, although it is tempting.

Update: The backlash for Big Ben's actions was severely delayed. The mainstream media almost had to be told when to go negative on Big Ben. Bloggers on the Internet had already scooped the mainstream press on most stories. Big Ben was finally suspended for 6 games (Four for Good Behavior).

Is Texas trying to Whitewash it's History???

As a Social Studies teacher, this story hit home. For those who don't know, Texas recently approved some changes to its social studies curriculum. Changes include:

- **Capitalism is now—Free enterprise system. (negative—Capitalist Pig)**
- **Thomas Jefferson is dropped because he coined the "separation of church and state" phrase.**
- **Efforts to include Hispanic/Latino heroes were defeated**
- **Students will now learn about the violent stance of the Black Panthers right along with the non-violent approach of MLK.**
- **NRA and Contract with america and other right wing political agendas are given spotlights.**
- **Stonewall Jackson, the Confederate general, is to be listed as a role model for effective leadership, and the ideas in Jefferson Davis' inaugural address are to be laid side by side with Abraham Lincoln's speeches.**
- **Country music is given special attention, while Rap music is omitted.**

What if this were to happen in Georgia? Or maybe South Carolina? Would kids start learning about the effectiveness of Governor Lester Maddox? (Some say he wasn't a racist because he had many black employees and nominated blacks in state govt during his administration.) Or "Pitchfork" Ben Tillman? I hope not. Let's keep partisan politics out of the classroom.

Double Edged Sword—The Role of the Media in Race Relations.

Timing is everything!!

Augusta is approaching the 40th year anniversary of the Race Riot of 1970. You would think that 40 years would be enough time for racial wounds to heal. But as you all know, if you pick at a scab, it will not heal properly. If you have a broken bone and you don't immobilize it, the bone may have to be reset. To apply this in real life terms, if people keep racially picking at open wounds, they will never heal. Let's put this in context according to the current climate in Augusta.

The community in Augusta is in crisis mode. Teen and gang violence have sent shock waves across the area. The deaths of local teens like Tykiah L. Palmer (with unborn child), and Brandon Taylor (both of Butler High School) have brought people together who care about our youth. I personally witnessed the outpouring of love and support at the Carrie J. Mays Community Center. Larry Fryer organized a wonderful program designed to make the community aware of ways they can help our young people. Supt. Dana Bedden, Minnesota Fattz, GA. Atty. General Thurbert Baker, and many other community leaders gave inspiring speeches to uplift the spirit of the community. All of this positive work being done in the community is very productive. Now let's jump to Monday, March 30th, 2010.

I was listening to the Austin Rhodes Show, (a local radio talk show, but influential amongst many in the Augusta area) and the conversation was centered on insensitivity. For some reason an e-mail came in and mentioned a skit from the Neil Boortz show called "Boo got shot". This skit featured an eyewitness account of a shooting in a black neighborhood where the young girl giving the account rambled on unintelligibly. It became obvious that they were reinforcing and making light of the stereotypes of uneducated black youth in the ghetto. Also the fact that someone was shot hardly seems to be a laughing matter considering the recent influx of teen and gang violence in the area. To put the cherry on top, they played a mix of the girl's interview set to rap music. Why does this even matter?

The media has a powerful influence on the racial climate in a community. If you have one side of town trying to provide a positive climate for our young people, and then on the other side of town they are making fun of the desperate plight of our young people, then a racial divide can set in.

I know some people may say: Why are you even listening to the Austin Rhodes show? Just turn the station!! Here is the problem. People's bosses, co-workers and schoolmates are listening to the Austin Rhodes Show. If we don't challenge and confront the source of many people's racist and stereotypical ideas, then how will the situation improve. I am not calling for a boycott of the Austin Rhodes Show, I just want them to know that there are some in the community who perceive skits like "Boo got shot" to be racially divisive and insensitive. And remember timing is everything. (remember the climate after 9/11)

Thanks to Austin Rhodes for reading my concerns on the air. (3/30/10)

Is the Tea Party Synonymous with Racism and Bigotry?

Much has already been written about the ignorant actions of a segment of the Tea Party. There are some who would argue that the Tea Party is nothing more than a dressed up version of the Klu Klux Klan. Some would argue that if you went to a Klan meeting a Tea Party might break out. Are people typecasting the Tea Party because of the racist actions of a few knuckleheads? Should those people be discounted as a fringe group who are not associated with the Tea Party movement?

People wouldn't categorize the Tea Party as racist if they would handle their business in-house. When racist actions occur within the Tea Party, the Tea Partiers should be the first to repudiate them. If you go to a rally and someone has a racist sign, then someone within the Tea Party should grab the sign and rip it up in their face and tell them they are not welcome to protest. (Maybe ripping the sign up is going too far, but they should find a civil way to tell the person, that their presence is not wanted.) If some idiot starts saying anything that could be perceived as racist, then they should tell them to go home. In other words, don't let a vocal minority dictate the image of your movement.

Instead of the actions that I described in the above paragraph, we get people in the Tea Party making excuses. We get people saying that the people who hurled racist epithets at black congressmen like Lewis (GA) and Cleaver (MO) were planted by democrats. Most people in the Tea Party have done everything but face the reality of racism within the movement. Remember the Black Panthers and the demise of Huey Newton. When those within the movement started to get involved in criminal activity, it wasn't long before the movement lost it's steam. I hope the same thing happens to the Tea Party movement. If your movement is not strong enough to expunge those weak minded individuals, then is it a movement worth having around?

I want to leave you with an experience that happened to me recently that illustrates my point. I posted a Yahoo article about the racist incidents that happened recently in D.C. A black lady named Veronica Foxx, a Tea Party supporter disputed the story. She said she was there and did not see or hear any reports of racist activity. She also said there were 30,000 people there. She refused to believe that people in the Tea Party could be so racist. I find that hard to believe since we are always seeing racist signs at these Tea Party rallies. She became so agitated that she accused me of being a racist for even bringing the matter up and disputing her claims. The final straw came when she said she was going to call my employer (Tutt middle school) and tell them they have a racist poisoning the young minds of Augusta, GA. That goes to show you how blind some people are to racism. I gave the lady my info and told her to go right ahead and make a fool of yourself, but she never called. With self-hating vindictive people like that representing the Tea Party, it's easy to see why people assume the worst when it comes to the Tea Party. as Rob Redding Jr. would say: Get off the Political Party Plantation, where's my whip, stuck on stupid, etc.

I went to a Klan Rally and a Press Conference broke out!!

For those who didn't know, there was a Klan rally in my former place of residence, Gloverville, S.C. The hype that led to the rally was big, but the end result was a sparse showing by the Klan. many excuses were made, but the verdict is in: The Klan is no Tea Party. Some suggested that if they called it a Tea Party instead of a Klan Rally, more people would have shown up.

When I first arrived I saw the bulk of the crowd keeping their distance, not wanting to be associated with the Klan. I saw a load of police and media, as well as people who wanted to show their opposition to the Klan. These people far outnumbered the Klan and its supporters. The focal point of the rally was supposed to be against illegal immigration and health care, but I did not hear any solutions or arguments against specific policy points. I expected to see white robes and plenty of rebel flags and signs, but I saw no robes and only one rebel flag.

It seemed that the organizer Tim Bradly wanted to show the face of the new Klan. He even suggested working with the NAACP. In a moment of manipulation, someone orchestrated a handshake between a young black man and the Grand Wizard Tim Bradly. After speaking with the young man, he expressed regret and felt that he could face retribution in Barton Village. (Barton Village is a predominantly black apartment complex in Augusta, GA) It was a sad case of how people manipulate images for their own leverage. The only place I saw the photo was in the Aiken Standard. Look closely at the picture and you will be able to see the bewilderment on the young man's face.

What's April Confederate History Month without talking about slavery?

When Virginia Governor Bob McDonnell declared April Confederate History Month, he opened up a can of worms. He further irritated people when he left out language concerning slavery. Many saw this as an attempt to whitewash the history of the motivations behind the Confederacy. Saying that the soldiers were fighting for states' rights, without saying that the major state right they were fighting for was the right to hold slaves, seems a little deceptive. I don't think anyone should demonize the Confederate troops, but to celebrate such an ugly time in U.S. History seems divisive.

More thought should have been given before making such a proclamation. You have to know that honoring the Confederacy would only serve to alienate many minorities. Maybe they should have a joint month to honor the Confederate History as well as those who opposed the evil institution of slavery. Whatever the case, something should be done to incorporate all ethnic groups into the fold. For Black History Month, it is also good to remember those who assisted the black community in their struggle for Civil Rights. In the same vein, Confederate History Month should include a place for those who were Southerners and opposed slavery and refused to support it. But to leave slavery out all together is unthinkable!!

Note: Virginia is not the only state to do this: Georgia, Texas and other southern states have had similar proclamations.

P.S.—Gov. McDonnell did go back and include language about slavery.

You would think that these two guys are still alive! Is the Civil War still being fought today? (art by Grady Abrams)

Black Expo in Savannah GA—(Savannah makes me Jealous)

Site of Black Expo-Savannah, GA

Today I went to the first annual Black Expo in Savannah at the convention center across the other side of the river. I always wondered what the inside looked liked. Every time I visited Savannah, it would be closed. I must say, the inside of the convention center was immaculate!! There were vendors from a variety of businesses set up. I even saw local businessman Mr. Hamilton from Hamilton Bookstore in Downtown Augusta with his own vending area. I even got to meet the Mayor of Savannah, Dr. Otis Johnson.

There were two panels set up for the day dealing with the State of Black America. Many prominent community leaders from the area were featured on the panel. The main attraction was Roland Martin, a frequent contributor on CNN and other media outlets. He even has his own show on TV One that features political guests. The discussion centered on the need to set a black agenda, health care, education as well as economic issues. The need for HBCU (*Historically Black Colleges and Universities*) support was also a hot topic. The second panel of the afternoon was more centered around entertainment issues and how it impacts our youth.

All in all, it was a beautiful day to be in Downtown Savannah. The waterfront was teeming with people, all ready to have a good time. Augusta should blatantly copy everything that Savannah has done with it's Riverwalk. We should have shops lining the river. We should have delicious restaurants right on the river. In other words, let's start developing directly on the river!!! I long to see the day when people from other areas come to the Riverwalk in Augusta and say: Man, I wish we had an area like this. North Augusta is pivotal in this development as well. Imagine a water taxi or ferry taking people from N. Augusta to Augusta and vice versa to shop and eat and play at various locations on the Savannah river. The possibilities are endless!!!

Butch Palmer, a community activist and businessman from the Harrisburg community in Augusta Georgia, made a controversial statement about Augusta "*turning into one big ghetto.*"

Here's a transcript of an exchange that I had with one of his supporters:

Plain Talk: Did Butch palmer make the statement Augusta is a big ghetto to get attention or was he really serious?

C. Mack: Better yet, what is YOUR opinion, Plain Talk?

Plain Talk: Get attention. He switched his support back to Matt A. overnight, when he said he was supporting the other candidate after Palmer lost. Hyperbole at its worst. If he keeps flip flopping it will be very hard to take him seriously. I don't know Mr. Palmer personally, so I won't readily deem his comments as racist. However they were very irresponsible, considering that the original ghettos were during the holocaust era.

C. Mack : "Well, of course he was not referring to the holocaust. And for your information, ghettos originated in Italy. It was were Jews were made to live about the 1700's, maybe a little earlier. The word is Italian. And perhaps you are the racist. The definition of ghetto is section of a city occupied by a minority group who live there especially because of social, economic, or legal pressure" NOT race or color. If people would read real books or real resources of information instead of solely relying on blogs and surfing and the media then maybe there would be less paranoia that everything a person says has to do with blacks and whites. You know if you want to really drag this nonsense out, bring up the word "African American." The way I see it if I call you (whomever) African American, then you better call me Scotch-Irish-Native American-Italian-Jewish-American."

Plain Talk: Thank you for enlightening me. However you seem to have misunderstood my statement. We live in the United States. Let's be honest with ourselves, when you think of the ghetto in the United States, what do you think of? Do you think about Italy? Do you really even think about Jews? His statement was irresponsible because he made a controversial statement without elaborating. How is Augusta becoming one big ghetto?

They are eliminating ghettos left and right in Augusta. Just ask MCG. Also, you committed the cardinal sin in discussing issues pertaining to race. You suggested that I may be racist. Ordinarily this is a conversation killer, but since I just wrote a book dealing with this very situation, I see where the problem lies. You don't know me, and I don't know you. Since you enlightened me on the origin of the word ghetto, let me enlighten you on the word racist. A racist believes that a person's race is the most important factor that determines that person's character and worth. They also believe that one race is superior to other races. How does that enter into our discussion? I said that I don't want to readily deem Mr. Palmer's comments as racist, even though most people associate ghetto with black. Please read my book Plain Talk. I talk about the danger of calling people racist. We can learn from each other if we really listen to one another. I don't have anything against Mr. Palmer, however he is a highly visible public figure and his words will be scrutinized more than others. I would like to firmly state for the record that I don't believe Mr. Palmer is a racist. I would like him to elaborate on his statement, because the media picks the most controversial sound bite to run with.

There have been many cases where I have had to personally apply the information in my book in dealing with others. This is just one case.

This is an exchange that I had with some Tea Party members in response to a report about Congressman John Lewis of Georgia being called the N-word at a Tea Party Demonstration in front of the Capitol. Notice how they make some tremendous assumptions. I never said that I was a democrat. I never said that I supported the Healthcare bill. I never called them names.

shirt being sold at Augusta Tea Party

(*This is the kind of extremist views that they espouse*)

Veronica Foxx: There were 35,000 people in attendance . . . the protest was Great expect for Jessie Jackson Jr. Out Of Every Congressman That Clown was The Worst . . . Mocking the crowds. IL should be forced to secede because of Obama and Jackson JR.

I started things off by merely posting a Yahoo report about the incident. I did not comment.

Veronica Foxx: Plain Talk: of course you believe anything about race because you're a leftist and that all you people see is race. However, I was there and

I've been at many protest for over this year and NEVER have I heard anyone yell "nigger." The only racism I've seen was at the 9.12 march when 4 black women rolled up in their car and called us name and spitted towards us. That's the only racism I've seen.

Plain Talk: You need to come to Georgia and see what I see. They are having a Klan Rally in Gloverville S.C. Walk around and tell me if you see racism. Some of these same people probably attend Tea Parties. Define Leftist. And then define socialist.

Plain Talk: Like you are supposed to hear someone yell the N-word. these cowards aren't that brave. They will only yell faintly enough for the intended target to hear them. Why would they let you hear it? It is only reserved for those that they disagree with.

Veronica Foxx: Plain Talk: In that case, how can Yahoo News hear it? Creditable Is LOST! you're telling me that I can't hear someone yell NIGGER yet Yahoo News can report on it?. Explain that?

Plain Talk: Cleaver was the one who heard it. Do you deny that there were people in the crowd saying inappropriate things? Instead of defending these people, you should be repudiating all forms of sexism, racism and all other isms. And just say anyone who says things like this is not a part of our movement. Instead we get people denying that things like this occur. Veronica, have you ever been called the N-word in derision?? If so, it is unmistakable. If not, then you are most fortunate, and it also may explain why we see things differently. I spoke to a white lady from N.J. and she couldn't believe that Klan rallies were still going on.

Joe Young: Plain Talk, you are a **lying racist TROLL . . . are you paid by ACORN?** LOL. When will you **lying parasites** get a conscience, Hmmmmm??? **How can you see the DIVERSITY at these tea Party rallies, then LIE about them being full of racists?? What is it like to LOOK IN THE MIRROR AND SEE A LIAR looking back??**

Brian Raben: I don't care what race or political party you are with there will always been a certain percentage of people that are racist. To suggest Tea Party people are racist more than someone else is just absurd.

Plain Talk: Joe define racist!! I wish I were being paid!!! You must be trembling right now with that vote coming up. It takes a big man for someone to call someone a liar that they have never met before. Simmer down, one way or another this will all be over and then you can get heated up over something else.

Plain Talk: Brian you are correct, but when people like Joe get heated up, sometimes the subconscious takes over. When that happens, you get a Kramer moment!!

Joe Young: **Corey Washington (a.k.a. Plain Talk) . . . it is truly pathetic that YOU, if you really are a 6th grade teacher, don't have the Character and INTELLECTUAL HONESTY to go to these rallies and SEE FIRST HAND what so many people of COLOR are doing there. Or DO YOU EVEN CARE about truth???**

Paul Younghaus: Plain Talk, get over it. Reading through this thread you don't want to listen to an on-the-spot witness like Veronica, you would rather listen to leftist drivel from media programmed to give you and Al Sharpton what you want. Yes there is prejudice around the world. Go to Afghanistan, China, Germany, and see if you don't feel some prejudice. Some of that is the chip on your shoulder. I've been to or lived in 126 countries, there is prejudice everywhere. But if you are a man, you will stand up for yourself, and render respect to others as you wish to receive yourself.

When you grow up, you may contact me!

Plain Talk: All of you are preaching to the choir, when someone mildly disagrees, you resort to name calling and cynical assumptions. If someone was heard on tape calling someone the N-word, then what would the excuse be. People are now saying that it was a plant.

Joe Young: It makes me **nauseous to think such a bigoted, disingenuous person stands in front of these children and brainwashes the children. For a TEACHER to say something as bigoted as there being a kkk rally "probably" some of them go to Tea Party rallies! " . . . probably."???** You "probably" don't know that Lincoln was a Republican, that the KKK was founded and filled with Democrats, and **Hillary, Bill and Barack IDOLIZE**

a Marxist radical named Saul Alinsky! Someone's been watching Glenn Beck and Fox News) Well . . . what do you care? You certainly don't care about INTELLECTUAL HONEST OR TRUTH.

Plain Talk: Are you Joe the plumber? You seem to know a lot about me. If you are so easily nauseous, then I feel sorry for you. Your rhetoric has escalated. You can't engage in a sensible debate. You feel that if I assassinate someone's character, it will make them go away. Then I can live happily ever after. Define bigot!! Define disingenuous!! Why do you assume that I am aligned with the Democrats?? Look over everything that I have written in my life and you will not find an endorsement of the healthcare bill or Democrats. Get off the political party plantation. stop slaving for partisans!! stop parroting talking points.

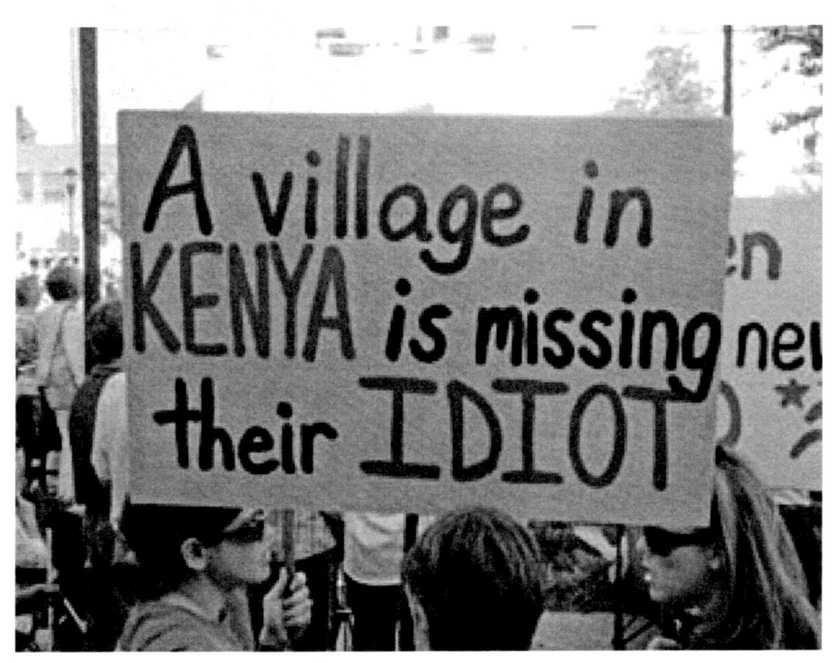

Signs with rhetoric like this, only serve to alienate people.

Joe Young: Corey Washington (a.k.a. Plain Talk) . . . HAH!!! TREMBLING?? The Supreme Court is licking their lips to get this Law contested for CONSTITUTIONALITY!! "Trembling"??? ROFL!! . . . you must be JOKING. A law SIGNED, and ESPECIALLY ONE OF THIS MAGNITUDE, will land if front of the Supreme Court before it is felt. ;-)

"Trembling"??? I am LAUGHING at the idea of the Dems committing political SUICIDE and getting voted out in November! LOL!!

O-Bow-ma is SO MANIACAL, he cannot even recognize he is destroying the credibility of his party for YEARS.

Please . . . PASS this bill!! PLEASE!!! LOL

Joe Young: "Sensible debate"?? Oh, you are also a comedian. Tell me the sense of a **"sensible debate" with a disingenuous person who won't even bother to SEE any Tea Party rallies where hundreds and thousands of PEOPLE OF COLOR attend of their own volition???** Hmmmm??? You are disingenuous, Mr. Washington . . . Go to these rallies AND TALK to the people of color who ATTEND. (I actually took his advice in Augusta-4/15/10) (Not much diversity at all!)

If . . . BIG IF . . . IF you are serious, then listen to the long list of black conservatives, and come back.

Joe Young: Corey Washington, I don't want you to go away. That is silly. I want you to stop being disingenuous in your presuppositions. Stay here and please find out why so many of **your fellow blacks** are in this movement. It is because they believe in individual liberty, personal integrity, individual accountability, self-determination in steering your own destiny. YOU, not the government, are responsible. These are just a few reasons . . . I can't name everything here and now . . . but talk to these people. Without bias . . . and see where they are coming from.

Paul Younghaus: Plain Talk, CF my previous comment and this, GROW UP. You are **black, get over it**. I didn't know I had something to get over??) If some dumb redneck in Tupelo, Mississipi says the N-word there, do you need to rise up like a Jihadist threatening death to a cartoonist in Denmark for making a cartoon of Allah? Or do you have enough intelligence to understand that not all that you read on the internet or the MSM is NOT TRUE? If you want to **race-bait**, you have lowered yourself. If you cannot stand alone as a man, and stand for yourself, I pity you. As my Gunnery Sergeant used to say of your like, you have elevated yourself to a position below whale dung, and are climbing lower. **I don't care what color**

you are, you are infatuated with it. And at the same time you **request "equality."** (*I have to actually request equality????*) If you want that then our color should not matter any more than yours, and a dumb redneck from Tupelo should not be a concern. Climb back up to the adult world and know that you can not make everyone like you, and it's not because you **happen to be black**.

Joe Young: Corey, what so often happens here in Facebook is that people come in with a chip on their shoulder to look to stir up trouble, and nothing else. I applaud you if you are sincerely interested in finding out what moves these people. But it tends to bring somebody out of his chair when somebody makes ludicrous claims. That is what happened, and I don't have a lot of patience at 3 AM (here in Germany) for such things. ;-)

Plain Talk: No problem Joe. I am not a partisan despite my stance on the Tea Party. I hope someone opens up a discussion to alternatives to Obamacare. (I know there are people pushing alternatives, but they are not widely known) I am late to the Healthcare debate. I do see an abundance of scare tactics. When I hear trigger words like—**Socialism, Fascism, Communism, Socialized Medicine**, it just makes me skeptical. Anyone who studies propaganda knows that you use words to sensationalize things. I saw this in too many discussions. I would have liked to have seen more energy expended by the Tea Party on alternatives. When you protest, people only see what you are against and not what you are for. Everybody seems to agree that health care needs to be reformed. As of right now, I will reserve judgment on the incident with Mr. Lewis until more info comes out. However, racism and slurs should not be taken lightly. It has led to violence in the past and it will lead to violence in the future.

I always learn from a hearty discussion with people that I disagree with. I usually let them vent and then cool off and then try to find common ground. If a person is reasonable, then they will at least be cordial.

Joe Young: I really don't understand you wishing people open something that is occurring all around you. It's THERE . . . you just have to go. Why won't you check out the Tea Party rallies? It is somewhat incomprehensible, seeing you are curious and some extremely sharp people—Blacks, Whites, Hispanic and others—attend and lead these things. I am so very impressed with so many truly brilliant black conservatives,—eloquent, lucent and inspiring

as MLK was. I still want to stand up and cheer when I hear MLK, . . . and I hear other blacks today that cause the same reaction. (*I wonder if MLK was alive today, would Joe be such a fan??*) No . . . they aren't AS inspiring as MLK, but almost. I been up all night. If you want, write me the next day or two, I will recommend some for you to check out.

Veronica Foxx: Everyone who thanked me for being there, MY PLEASURE! I keep thinking about all the patriots nationwide who couldn't be there. Plain Talk I lived in GA for 7 yrs so what town is the KKK Rally? **I have a hard time believe a racist such as yourself. The most racist group in America are blacks because they NEVER check their prejudices at the door and thinks its ok For them to be racist because of "what the white man did to us" THAT'S DUMB! (*This is a black lady trying to score brownie points with her Conservative friends.*)** Conservatives, for the most part, don't see race we just want our country back on track THAT'S IT! Cory notice that **its ALWAYS Dems that bring up race . . . it's because you and the Dems are racist. I'm not saying racism doesn't exist but so the heck what?** (Very sad statement)

By the way, It's you that can look at a crowd of white people and assume that they are racist. That's because you have hate in your heart for white

people. ***(Taken from the Glenn Beck Playbook) (Obama has a hatred for white people statement)*** **Again, there are blacks Mexican, Asians and every other race at the tea parties.**

Pray for yourself. (She had to try and interject religion into the debate) (I wasn't going to go there, but Oh well, here it goes!)

Plain Talk: Please define racist. It's an overused word like socialism and fascist. The rally is in Gloverville, S.C. (as a teen walking down the street I was called the N-word by a little boy who was coached to do so by his father. I just shook my head and kept walking) which is in Aiken Co., they also had a Klan Rally in south Georgia. They have had a Tea Party Rally here in Augusta.(all white except for a black man that they bused in to entertain the crowd) (I was referring to an earlier Tea Party where the video was posted on-line) I know it's painful for those who are partisan to hear, but the Tea Party has not distanced itself from racists. A little leaven ferments the whole lump. Veronica your words are filled with stereotypes. I hear many talking points in your responses. I get the eerie feeling that I have heard these words before on some conservative talk show. Race is brought up because it is still relevant. Marginalizing it only makes it worse. Repudiating it every chance you get unequivocally is the only Christian thing to do. Would Jesus be proud of some of the things said at that rally yesterday? Would he be rallying with you or staying out of the fray. Remember the people tried to make Jesus a King. He said: My kingdom is no part of this world. Remember when someone wanted to involve Jesus in an inheritance dispute. Jesus wanted no part of it. If the bill passes, so be it. If it fails, so be it. I won't lose sleep. I am still finding it hard to believe that some of you got so worked up over the mild things that I said. I did not attack anyone. I did not call anyone a racist. I even said that I would reserve judgment on the Lewis story until more info came out. This still was not enough for some people. How can you engage in debate when you are calling people racist without proof. Who is the god of this system of things? (2 Corinthians 4:4) (**I should be staying out of this whole political mess**) (It's a dead end!)

(When you go back at people with religion they seem to lose it at that point)

Veronica Foxx: Plain: **Jesus doesn't know a racist such as yourself so don't bring him into the picture as your defense. You're not worth debating with because you have your racist mind made up that a black man was**

bused in to be made fun of at the tea parties!! what proof do you have of that? As for talking points NO SIR i don't need talking point because I have self evident truth. I've lived in SC and GA and again **most of the racist people are Black.** PEROID you can't fool me. Furthermore ***if I find out what school you teach at I'm going to call them and ask why they have a racist such as yourself teaching kids.***

As a matter of fact, I'll make it my goal to do just that.

Have a good one.

(This lady has lost her mind. She is so lofty and blindly partisan that she wants to call from Washington D.C. to Augusta Ga, and bother people about her warped political views. Even after reading over my statements, I still don't see anything that would disqualify me from working with kids. Everybody wants to be a Supt., but nobody wants to get their hands dirty in the classroom. Conservatives are supposed to be for local control of education, what would this lady add to the conversation about the education of kids here in Augusta???)

Joe Young: Plain Talk, . . . do you have a video of this so-called rally?

Post the link. No video? Then you are lying. (I posted the video later) you are losing credibility every time you open your mouth. Your incindiary comments just keep rolling. You aren't interested, as you now prove, in dialogue, . . . you only are interested in BAITING.

You are, in my eyes now, a follower of **Alinsky**. This is my last response. (another Fox News talking point)

(This guy is a piece of work!! He speaketh in riddles!!)

Paul Younghaus: Plain talk, I have a video from a Tea Party that has a lot of racism in it, it's a speech by Alfonso Rachel, a man who I've subscribed to for about four years, before Obamacare! You want to hear some "plain talk" listen to this:

(He posted a Youtube video of a black guy in Dallas named Zoe giving a speech at a Tea Party Rally. Zoe said Democrats were pushing racism and the Tea Party is not racist. The crowd seemed to mistrust him. It was very bizarre.)

The preceding people are on what Rob Redding Jr. would call "The Political Party Plantation". These are people who are slaves to a political ideology. They regurgitate talking points fed to them by political operatives and pundits. True sycophants.

Sycophants: servile self-seekers who attempt to win favor by flattering influential people.

Check out the following essay to further illustrate what I am talking about.

Political Party Plantation (courtesy of Rob Redding Jr.)

In a political bombshell book called Game Change, it was revealed that Sen. Harry Reid of Nevada privately expressed that Barack Obama would win the White House the because he is a "light skin African American with no Negro dialect, unless he wanted to have one". This statement embarrassed many people in the Democratic Party. Many consider this a major distraction while a massive health-care reform bill was trying to be passed in Congress. Many Republicans including GOP Chairman Michael Steele cried double standard because of the treatment of former GOP Republican leader Trent Lott, when he spoke favorably of Sen. Strom Thurmond's positive stance on segregation. When Mr. Lott made the statements, an uproar in the Democratic community was made. Many African-Americans in the Republican Party also were disturbed by comments made by Mr. Lott. There was pressure within the Republican Party for influential minorities such as Colin Powell, Sec. of Educ. Rod Paige, and Condoleezza Rice to publicly back Trent Lott. But this did not happen. All of this hoopla eventually led to Trent Lott's resignation.

Did this man's light skin and dialect influence your vote? Harry Reid thinks so!!

What about the Democrats? Surely they would not hold back from telling it like it is. Since many of these Democrats were so highly offended in Trent Lott's comments, they must also be disturbed at Sen. Reid's comments. Sadly, this was not the case. Pres. Obama quickly came out and forgave Sen. Reid and said "the book is closed". House majority whip Jim Clyburn of South Carolina, the highest ranking African-American in Congress has been known to speak out on matters of racial issues. He led the charge to censor representative Joe Wilson of South Carolina for his inappropriate outburst of "you lie" during the president's State of the Union address. Mr. Clyburn also spoke out against Bill Clinton's comments belittling Obama's win in South Carolina, where Bill Clinton compared Obama's win with Jesse Jackson's win in South Carolina. However, in Sen. Reid's case, Mr. Clyburn came out immediately in support of Sen. Reid. What about Al Sharpton? Would he have some biting criticism for Sen. Reid? Based on his treatment of the Don Imus situation where he called for Imus to be fired, and his harsh criticism of Gilbert Arenas, you would think Sharpton may even call for Sen. Reid's resignation. Instead Sharpton mildly said that "Reid did not select the best word choice in this instance". Sharpton did not call for Reid's resignation. Not by a long shot! Going a step further, DC political leader Eleanor Holmes Norton, chose to speak for all black people when she said that the opponents of Sen. Reid "will not find a welcome mat in the black community", if they try to make a big deal out of Reid's comments.

What is really disappointing is that the impetus of the discussion lies with whether Reid should step down or saying that Reid's comments are not as bad as Trent Lott's. What the conversations should focus on is what Reid's words really say about his character. In Reid's mind, if Barack Obama was dark skinned, he would have not been president. If Barack Obama's language skills were lacking, he would not be president. I can see the latter point, but Reid chose to say "Negro dialect". What is "Negro dialect"? I have heard of a Southern dialect, but never a Negro dialect. There are many black people that may not have a proper command of the English language, but the same can be said of people of any race. What makes an elderly white gentleman from Nevada an expert on black linguistics? Is speaking proper English "White dialect"?

Sen. Reid's words reflect a backward way of thinking. Ever since slavery days, slaves were pitted against one another based on the color of their skin. The lighter skinned slaves were taught that they were better, and they were even treated better. Often times lighter skinned slaves' language skills were better than the darker slaves' skills because of their close proximity to their master's house. Sen. Reid's comments hearken back to a dark period in American history. Negro dialect, according to Reid, is inferior to White dialect. There is a common stereotype of African-Americans that states: black people cannot speak proper English. If you are black and speak properly, some may even accuse you of trying to be white. This is not an idea just pushed by white racists. The notion of proper speech being exclusive to whites is embraced by many in the black community as well. What we need to do is examine our own internal biases and stereotypes in order to ask ourselves: Am I striving to be the best I can be when it comes to my command of the English language? Whatever country you are a citizen of, should motivate you to speak that language properly. That is about the best any of us can do.

You may be wondering by now why I named this section "Political Party Plantation". According to Rob Redding Jr., who has written a book called Hired Hatred, political party affiliation has trumped common decency and common sense. When people become loyal Democrats or loyal Republicans, they become slaves to their party's platform. Those people who are on the "Political Party Plantation" will spin any event in order to make their party look good. This is very unfortunate and inconsiderate considering the magnitude of the issues that politicians have to deal with.

Here's an interview I did with J.J. Gaines for the Call and Post out of Cleveland Ohio:

- **What inspired you to write Plain Talk?**
  A series of events that occured in the summer of 09'. You had the arrest of Henry Louis Gates Jr. In Cambridge and the whole notion of race in that episode. There was also a moving Series on CNN called Black in America 2, this provided many positive stories to make me want to do something positive. At the same time I also was reading an article on discrimination that was from a religous standpoint, showing how this was not the Creator's intention for us to live this way. All these things spurred me to want to write a book that will help people understand each other. There was also a call from the mainstream media to open up a fresh dialog on race.

- **How did you come up with the title?**
  The Title Plain Talk came from my frustration in reading books on Race. Many of them approached Race from a scientific or academic standpoint. That limits your audience. I wanted to write a book that intentionally speaks to a wide range of people, without dumbing anything down. I

am not trying to impress people with big words, but this book will make you think.

- **When did you first consider yourself a writer?**
  In school they used to always make us write. In college, the writing became more intense. Let's face it, if anyone desires to better themselves in life, you have to be a prolific writer. Especially with e-mails in full use. Writing is the most prominent mode of communication for most people living in a fast paced world. But to answer your question directly, I would say my last year in college going for my 4 yr. Degree. It was writing assignment after writing assignment. That is when I realized, this writing thing, I'll be doing this for a while.

- **What books have most influenced your life most?**
  The Bible is the only book that I read everyday without exception. I have already read it from cover to cover twice. As far as secular books, I remember reading Animal Farm and being blown away with the concept. I was interested in the various theories about the book. The book taken at face value shows how things can change those with good intentions. Also my essay on Animal Farm, helped get me a full scholarship with the Dept. Of Agriculture in D.C.

Picture of me receiving certificate, from former Sec. of agriculture, Mike Espy, for scholarship to S.C. State in Washington D.C.

- **If you had to choose, which writer would you consider a mentor?**
  Michael Eric Dyson—I tend to gravitate towards his books. He writes on a wide variety of subjects. He puts his soul into his writings. He is not afraid to critique his own flaws. He also can make you laugh from time to time.

- **What book are you reading now?**
  I am reading some books on Hispanic culture. One is called His**panic** by Geraldo Rivera. It shows how the U.S. Is afraid of the Hispanic influx into this country. Another is Spanglish by Ed Morales. It really brings to light many issues in the Hispanic community and how they have also had to deal with stereotypes and discrimination. They also have issues about what to call themselves and light skin vs. dark skin conflicts. I saw many similarities with the Black community.

- **What are your current projects?**
  I am compiling research for my second volume of Plain Talk, tentatively titled: Digging a little Deeper. There are so many events happening at such a fast pace, it's hard to decide which ones to select.

- **Do you see writing as a career or a hobby?**
  Right now I see it as a hobby. I am a middle school teacher in Augusta Georgia at Tutt middle. That is my main job. I would like to write as a full time job, so I hope that the Plain Talk Series catches on. Either way, it's been fun.

- **If you had to do it all over again, would you change anything in your latest book?**
  I designed the cover, but a graphic artist took my primative drawings and produced a professional looking cover. These people are in the Phillipines, so they may have misunderstood me. I wanted the cover to reflect two different races talking to each other. A black male and a white woman, or vice versa. I still get positive compliments on the cover, so I am satisfied.

- **Do you recall how your interest in writing originated?**
  In college when they would let us choose our own topics, I would always choose topics that would stay with me. I remember choosing a Vietnam theme that encouraged me to learn more about the Vietnam experience. One of my favorite papers that I did was on Jimi Hendrix. I examined why he was not appriecated in the Black community. Doing specific historical topics, peaked my interest in writing non-fiction. I could care less about writing fiction.

- **Can you share a little of your current work with us?**
  I have a section in Volume 2 called: Lost in Translation. This is where I talk about situations where many people may scream racism, but can you dig deeper to see if there are other more indicating factors. Like, if I go to the fancy part of town and I am dressed a certain way, more than likely many people will treat me differently. Is that race or class distinction? If I were to go to that same area dressed in a designer suit and get treated nicely, then we know it wasn't race. But, If I go back in a suit and the people treat me in the same way that they treated me when I was dressed poorly, then there may be some racial issues. This piece is just designed to have people look at Racism as the last resort.

- **Is there anything you find particularly challenging in your writing?**
  It is hard to stay up to date and relavent with racial issues. By the time you go to print, many of the stories may have fizzled out. That's why you have to select stories that can be used to represent larger issues. I wrote about Mike Vick and Kanye West, these two stories are still on-going. We still don't know how they will turn out.

- **Who is your favorite author and what is it that really strikes you about their work?**
  Right now John McWhorter is my favorite. What strikes me about his work is that he can not be boxed in to a category. One minute you are disagreeing with him. The next minute you are totally argeeing with him. He forces you to think on your toes when you are reading.

- **Do you have anything specific that you want to say to your readers?**
  I would like to thank everyone that has read my book for supporting an unknown author. I hope that you will share this book with your kids and other family members. Many of our kids are growing up in

a world riddled with bad habits left to them by adults. Let's focus on the mistakes that we have made in order to make sure that our children don't continue to pass these bad habits to their kids. If Richard Pryor can stop saying the N-Word, then so can you.

- **What was one of the most surprising things you learned in creating your books?**
  If you want to know who your friends are, then write a book. You will have those who you thought were cool with you say things behind your back. They will belittle your accomplishments. They will get the sudden urge to want to write a book of their own. I am glad that they exposed themselves. I just take their negativity and use it to fuel my creativity.

CHAPTER TWO

Contemplating Deep Social Issues

This chapter will focus on issues that continue to plague society. Even if you don't believe that society can solve these problems overall, it's still good to think deeply about these issues, so that you can help those in your immediate circle.

ABCs of Racial Rapport

When dealing with people of various races, it is always good to have a certain mindset. In order to have this mindset, we have to prepare our minds. That is why I have created this acrostic to trigger the memory, when it comes to building a rapport with other races. This acrostic applies to all races, because we all want to be treated with respect, no matter our race. This acrostic is very Self-Help based, because what you get out of it, depends on your ability to meditate and apply yourself to each alphabet. I am sure you can think of some additional points to include:

A is for Attitude—It can say a great deal about how you feel about other races. They pick up on your attitude and are always checking to see if it is different around other races.

B is for Behavior—Another indicator that people pick up on is your behavior. Do you behave differently around other races? Is it noticeable?

C is for Context and Connotation—Your words can easily be taken out of context when dealing with other races due to **that other C word—Culture**. Also watch the connotation of your words. For instance: monkey, gorilla, banana, fried chicken, watermelons, these words are harmless by themselves. But when you use them a certain way referring to people of color, then things can get dicey. (See Volume 1 for examples galore) (Also ask Dan Rather about watermelons)

D is for Diversity—Get to know people of other races and cultures. Truly accept them for who they are.

E is for Education—When people accurately educate themselves about other races and cultures, it cuts down on the stereotyping. You are not relying on the biases of others to dictate your cultural knowledge.

F is for Free—as in free your mind of all the garbage floating around about other races. The media is a major culprit in disseminating seemingly innocuous stereotypes of all races. Take each person on an individual basis to avoid embarrassing situations.

G is for Gravitate—If you project yourself as a person who treats all races fairly and evenly, then like-minded people will naturally gravitate towards you.

H is for Hatred, Harbor, and Hostility—These are strong words, but they can easily seep into our lives if we are met with extreme circumstances. Many people remember what someone of a particular race has done to them or a loved one, and they held the entire race accountable for the actions of one or a select few.

I is for Investigate—Discover positive exploits of people of various races. You may develop new found respect for a wide variety of races. People of all races have made positive contributions to the betterment of life.

J is for Justify—as in don't justify any racist actions or beliefs of yourself or any other person. It is easy to find ourselves making excuses, especially when the offender is a close friend or family member. We want to give people the benefit of the doubt, but if you continue to justify racist behavior and speech, then you are not helping the person you are justifying.

K is for Knowledge—Becoming knowledgeable about other races and cultures equips you to not only relate and understand other people, but it also allows you to spread your knowledge to others. We are not talking about mere facts and statistics, but information that is personal and practical.

L is for Limited—We don't want to become limited in our thinking, choice of friends, choice of activities, etc. It can be very tempting to stay within your comfort zone. What if Jimi Hendrix would have stuck solely to playing R&B music? What if the Beatles would have just stayed in England?

M is for Media Manipulation—Sensationalism and negativity sells. No matter what people say, they gravitate toward these things. Make no mistake, the media loses more and more integrity every single day. Journalism is a very competitive field, and many times the bottom line takes precedent over what's right or beneficial for people to see or hear. The media sometimes stokes the racial flames in order to get ratings/attention. In Plain Talk Vol. 1, I bring out how many people get their ideas of other races from their entertainment, which in most cases is covered by the media. Please recognize where you are being manipulated and don't fall for the old okey-doke!

N is for the other N-word—Negativity—It is so easy to think negatively about someone who looks different than we do. They may have cultural ways that seem weird or idiosyncratic, or other aspects about them that we can take the wrong way. Just like we look at Asians sideways for eating dogs and cats, other cultures are probably miffed at some of the things that we do here in the United States.

O is for Optimistic—which is what you must remain when it comes to your stance on race relations. Other people need to follow your cue, and not the other way around. It may take other people a while to come around to your positive attitude, but don't give in to the air of racial negativity and pessimism in the world. People are commenting all the time in the form of gripes and complaints. There is a time for that, but don't let it overtake your ideals and aura. The Internet is a prime example of a place where people find it easy to hide behind a computer and spew racial bigotry and hatred. Sometimes you just have to stop reading comments and move on.

P is for Practice what you Preach—when people hear that you are speaking out against racism, they will be watching you closely to see if you follow your own advice. **P is also for Prepared** . . . as in be prepared to defend yourself. When it comes to race, people are easily offended and their response mechanism is to become defensive. Be prepared for someone to lash out at you. They may even try to turn the tables and call you a racist. Just stay calm and collected and find out why the person feels that way. Once they see your cool approach, they may feel bad about lashing out. That is your opportunity to reason with the person and find common ground.

Q is for Quirk—People of other races may have peculiar traits or idiosyncrasies. You may even think that they are downright eccentric. But just think . . . they may feel the same way about you!

R is for Rapid, Reflex, Reactionary, and Response—Do you react impulsively to matters of race? Do you take time to look at multiple perspectives when it comes to race and culture? Do you have a knee-jerk defensive response when it comes to defending your race? We don't want to be impulsive or driven by instinct when it comes to race. It is hard to think things through when we allow our subconsciousness to take over. That's how so many of the celebrities that I talk about in Plain Talk Volume One got in trouble. (Examples: Michael Richards, Dog the Bounty Hunter, possibly even Kanye West and Serena Williams)

S is for Super Sensationalism—Be aware of hidden agendas of not only the media, but simple word of mouth. Why is this person saying this about that person? Is it really as bad as they make it out to be? It must be something that they are leaving out.

S is also for Sensitive Sensibilities—We have to examine ourselves. Do we allow slights to sour our perceptions of entire races? Why didn't they include a Black, White, or Hispanic? That's not fair! They wouldn't have treated me like that if I were White/Black/Asian! Don't get me wrong, discrimination occurs on a daily basis. Just make sure you look at the totality of the situation and not cast aspersions on entire races. Also, don't impugn wrong motives without fully knowing all of the facts.

T is for Trust and Time—Trust that staying the course will be beneficial. Despite attempts to think negatively or get into racial bickering, give your new approach some time. Both for yourself, to see the benefits, and for those around you, to see that you are not trying to be a phony. The events of racial hurt interwoven into the fabric of the world have developed a strong sense of mistrust in people. It will take time for some to see that you are the real deal when it comes to building a good racial rapport.

U is for Understanding and Unwavering—You must develop understanding when it comes to race. It will take time and you may encounter resistance. It will take understanding to forgive and forget when others verbally (and in some cases physically) attack you for being a peacemaker. One of the tenants of the civil rights movement was to not hate your attacker. Instead, you should feel empathy and sympathy for that person. That is why many years later, many civil rights activists who were attacked viciously by misguided people were able to forgive them freely. When this occurs, it is amazing the level of remorse that those attackers have. So you must be unwavering in your resolve.

V is for Venom—which racist will spew. But **V is also for vindication** if you see your way through. **(I'm a poet and didn't know it)**

W is for Willpower—You will need willpower to keep your cool in the face of insults and the assassination of your character. You will also need willpower to respond with a mild disposition.

X is for Xenophobia—despite all of the talk of immigration, illegal aliens, border patrol, and Islamic terrorists, stay clear of xenophobic comments and attitudes. Don't believe the hype!!

Y is for Yielding—You have to be flexible and not insist on the superiority of your own culture. If you are rigid and stiff in your assertions, it will most certainly lead to friction and conflict.

Z is for Zenith—which is what you can reach with respect to your rapport with other races and cultures . . . If you practice and preach the ABCs of racial rapport.

Rebuttal for the Argument of Genetics being a direct link to Intelligence with respect to Race.

The genetic argument for linking race and intelligence is made to be very complex. Some try to explain that black children perform more poorly than white children in school based solely on genetics. To prove this theory, they make the over-simplified observation that everywhere you go, you see blacks forming an underclass of society in whatever country you happen to be in. But one has to ask the question, is this genetics or just flat-out racism? When I say racism, I'm talking about institutionalized racism. Racism that has been perpetuated for centuries, if not millenniums. In order to convince themselves that genetics plays a role, these people make a sharp distinction between North Africa and the rest of Africa. This is a big sticking point for this argument, because most people know Egypt as being one of the first true great centers for learning. In fact, Egypt is where many Greeks built upon their knowledge. Maybe I'm getting ahead of myself. Let's start this rebuttal from a common ground. We will reference the book that got everyone talking in 1994: The Bell Curve-Intelligence and Class Structure in American Life. This book was written by Richard J. Herrnstein, a professor of psychology at Harvard, and Charles Murray, a Harvard graduate and a research fellow at the American Enterprise Institute.

Before The Bell Curve was written, there were similar people who may similar arguments. In 1969, Arthur Jensen stated that remedial programs do not help disadvantaged children, because of their low IQ. Another trial blazer in this train of thought was William Shockley, who was a Nobel Laureate in physics. His highly educated mind came up with the diabolical idea to pay people with low IQ scores to be sterilized. The book The Bell Curve repeated the ideas of these two men by suggesting that low IQ people were the ones who were having most of the babies, thus dragging America down. When you break it down, the book The Bell Curve was nothing more than one giant advertisement for eugenics. For those who don't know, eugenics is the study and practice of selective breeding applied to humans, with the aim of improving the species. The main reason why eugenics is heavily frowned upon, has to do with its connections to Nazi Germany.

The authors of The Bell Curve painstakingly tried to use statistics to link low IQ scores with poverty, unemployment, criminal activity, and ultimately race. Then for some strange reason, they try to make a huge jump and say that low IQ scores are mainly determined by genetics, and to a lesser extent by the person's environment. As an interesting side note, The Bell Curve shows that Ashkenazi Jews of European origin and East Asians (Chinese and Japanese) scored higher on IQ tests than American whites. This information was mainly ignored by many people, because then you would have to promote Jews and Asians as being the superior races. Instead, what was focused on was the placement of blacks to the lower end of the genetic lottery.

The New York Times brought out that one of the authors, Charles Murray, went on a cross burning spree with his friends in Iowa. Murray claims that as a high school senior at that time, he was unaware of the racist nature of the cross burnings. How ironic, coming from a man writing a book belittling the intelligence of entire races of people. It's hard to believe that people would go around burning crosses and not engage in any racist dialogue.

Richard A. Gardner, a noted professor of child psychology at Columbia University, did not agree with the premise of The Bell Curve. He said that IQ test merely measured how well you have learned what is taught in school. In fact, according to Gardner, IQ tests are not a measure of intelligence, but rather a measure of educational performance. Gardner went on to suggest a proper name for IQ tests: "they would be called: Tests that predict success or failure in the school system from which the questions have been derived".

In other words, a positive family and school environment translates into high IQ scores. Race has nothing to do with high IQ scores. It just so happens that a large majority of minorities are missing this positive family and school environment. It could be poverty, one parent households, inferior schools, etc., that caused minorities to score low on IQ tests. (Insert black or African American in the place of minorities) The institution of racism still exists, in that schools in more affluent neighborhoods are better than schools in rural or poor inner-city neighborhoods. I don't want to hear how much the schools in Washington DC spend per pupil, because when you are going to school in an unsafe environment, learning drops off dramatically. Throwing more money at schools does not make them better. You have to have the total package. You need proper funding for materials, as well as great teachers, but there are also other intangibles that have nothing to do with money. For instance, good parent-teacher relationships, a safe learning environment, positive school culture, and business/community involvement.

The institution of racism sees to it that minorities have a hard time finding many jobs, bank loans, etc. It is a vicious web that must be removed, a cycle if you will, that must be broken. Individuals who are minorities can and do beat many of these factors. My question is: How do you level the playing field for all people? Affirmative action is good for some, but not adequate. It is up to each individual to find a way to overcome any obstacle that stands in their way. I'm not excusing those who continue to push the institution of racism, I'm just saying that you should anticipate racial obstacles if you are a minority and find a way to not only overcome those obstacles, but shatter any myths, stereotypes, or biases toward you as a minority. That is not trying to be white, but trying to be the best person that you can possibly be. Harvard psychiatrist Alvin Poussaint, said it would only be fair to compare apples to apples by taking a group of white people that have gone through 250 years of slavery, 100 years of Jim Crow, and then compare the IQ scores of those white people to black people. We know that you will not find a group to do the test study with, so his point is well taken.

Trying to say that intelligence and cognitive abilities are genetic is a nice way to justify the institution of racism. It is a way to excuse the many years of European imperialism and exploitation. Saying that blacks are in their current position because of their genes, heritage, behavior, and culture; and leaving out European misconduct (i.e.: slavery, Jim Crow, lynchings, institutional racism) is a pipe dream for many white people. I'm not saying that we should use the race card to play upon "white guilt". I'm just saying, please don't insult my intelligence and demean me with silly theories of racial superiority. There are too many outlying factors that come into play. The way things are now with respect to the disparity of the achievement gap between white and black people, can be traced back throughout history. But you don't want to do well on the past to the point where it paralyzes you now. So let's just see how we can work together by improving relations now and removing the last vestiges of institutionalized racism. This probably can't be done on a worldwide level, but it can be done on an individual level. Or even better, if you have power or authority over other people, your sphere of influence will be wider.

To sum up, we know there are tremendous obstacles to minority groups as a whole, but there are mechanisms in place in which to utilize, to give yourself a fighting chance. Why not use your abilities to move ahead and help others who have been in a similar situation. Making excuses only keeps you in the same place. That goes for both sides, both white and black, and everyone in between.

Entrapment of African Americans-Is the Man out to get us?

Over the years, many African-Americans both famous and not famous, have been entrapped by law enforcement. I am sure you know of many stories in your local area, of black political officials being set up by law enforcement. In the Augusta area, we had former mayor Ed McIntyre, and state representative Charles Walker involved with the authorities. More well-known cases would probably include: former mayor of Washington DC, Marion Barry, O.J. Simpson, Michael Vick, Michael Jackson, and Kobe Bryant. I'm not saying that all of these individuals were set up by sting operations, but they all have been at odds with the law. In each case there has been some controversy as to whether or not they were targets because of being powerful black men.

The truth of the matter is, with race not being discussed openly, it allows for wounds to never heal. It always seems that the white power structure wants to bring down powerful black man. Since the FBI or other law-enforcement agencies are usually run by whites, this blinds the minds of many African-Americans. Another sticking point with black people would be the fallacy of the American justice system in dealing with blacks in the past. Many African-Americans still remember the lack of justice during the civil rights era. With that being said, many blacks feel that it is their obligation to support their "brother in need". Black solidarity with knowledge of the history of the lopsidedness of the American judicial system, always trumps the wrongdoings of any African American male that is set up by a sting operation or accused of wrongdoing by whites. Unfortunately, those who have committed those wrongs know that, and use the situation to their full advantage. If you are a powerful black male, how can you see a trap, fall in the trap, and then blame it on someone else.

Keeping with the tradition of the Plain Talk series, let's make sure that we are on the same page here:

Is the Man out to entrap me? If that's what you really think, then why fall for the trap?

***Definition of entrapment*—the action of luring an individual into committing a crime in order to prosecute the person for it.**

You may say, the outrage is in the selectiveness of the white power structure in their targeting of black males. However, white politicians and other figures fall prey to FBI setups all the time. If you are an honest individual, it shouldn't matter what they throw at you. You should pass the test and then play the "victim" card. You shouldn't fall for the trap, get caught, and then scream racism and entrapment, and try to play the "race" card.

There are actual cases where the government is dead wrong in trying to lure people into committing crimes. There are laws on the books for that! But many cases of so-called entrapment are just people with bad morals or motives who took the bait and got caught.

White Privilege—Fact or Myth?

Some people believe that White people are afforded many advantages in the world based solely on the color of their skin. Comedians such as Eddie Murphy, Richard Pryor, and Dave Chapelle have often taken lighthearted jabs at this. But is there some validity or truth to the theory of White Privilege? Obviously, I'm not saying that White people have conspired to give each other breaks or advantages, but rather, my assertion is that there are vestiges of an institution that favors the dominant culture. As you read over the following paragraphs, mentally check to see if it would be just as easy for a person of color in these situations.

Access to higher education—*Do White people have access to better schooling?*

In a sense, yes. But only because of the gap in income. Those people of color who do have access to money, have taken advantage of higher education just as much as Whites. Also those people of color who are poor, but highly motivated in the pursuit of their education, always seem to find a way to advance. Either through Pell grants, student loans, or scholarships, they will find a way. So the only truth to this White Privilege of access to better education has to do with money and the White culture stressing education. That means that the Black community needs to work harder to change their overall cultural stance on education. A paradigm shift if you will, of epic proportions. Little Black kids should see getting a good education as the primary means of bettering their life, and not selling drugs, playing sports, or getting into show business.

Better job opportunities/advancement—*Do White people have easier access to better jobs and promotions than people of color?*

Something could be said for black people not being prepared, but what if they are qualified and still are passed over for promotions? Unfortunately, this does happen enough for many people to take notice of it. Not just black people, but women and other ethnic groups have complained about the "good ole' boy" system that solely caters to White men. People often cite the US history of presidential elections as proof of the propensity to recognize White males as leaders of this country. The same percentage holds true in terms of CEO's and upper management. Despite everything I just said, this still doesn't negate the responsibility to be prepared, just in case your name is called. It's just like the reserve player in sports, who rarely sees playing time. If there are a few injuries, then you may be called on to start or play big minutes. If you are not prepared, then you have blown your opportunity to show off your skills. If you are prepared at all times and perform well, then you will have a better chance of prospering. You never know who is watching!

Do white people have greater access to ________________.

By now you can see it doesn't matter what you put in the blank, it all boils down to a few factors: *money, money, and more money.* In a capitalist society, money affords you many privileges. So I think the deeper more probing question that many Black people should have is: Why are people of color as a whole on the bottom of every aspect of prosperity. High crime rates, low life expectancy, poverty, poor health care, etc. Some of these factors are due to outright racism and discrimination, but the majority of these issues are self-inflicted.

As a teacher, I see firsthand the treatment of education in the Black community. I see kids coming to school without supplies, without respect, and without homework. I see parents coming to conferences and making excuses, and some just telling us what we want to hear. Of course, these actions are not restricted to Black parents, but it's always the Black kids who come out the biggest losers in this grand scheme of education. I see kids who haven't passed a test all year, recite rap songs with perfect recollection. I see kids who have not turned in homework all year long, come to school and talk about how many video games they have. Am I talking exclusively about Black kids. Absolutely not! But once again, Black kids can ill afford to coast when it comes to their education. So the last thought that I would like to stress to all communities, but especially the Black community is: *Please place a greater emphasis on education and don't let your kids put it in cruise control at school.* Because the rest of the world has their pedal to the metal when it comes to their education. **(I know that sounded corny, but give me a break! I'm talking to the kids.)**

Is Blackface making a Comeback?

In Plain Talk Volume One, I brought out how minstrel shows contributed to the reinforcement of negative black stereotypes. In these minstrel shows, white men would perform in blackface, while exaggerating the mannerisms of black people. With the progression of society and the ability of black folk to have more control of their image, blackface and minstrel shows went the way of the Dodo (extinct). But with the election of the first black president, is blackface trying to make a comeback?

You would think so, with the rash of situations involving blackface recently. Let me be clear of what I mean when I say "blackface". Blackface is not merely a white person putting on makeup to artistically transform into a black person. (i.e.: Saturday Night Live's Fred Armisen's portrayal of Pres. Obama) Blackface is usually exemplified by mocking the speech or behaviors of black people, in a way that is offensive, stereotypical, and sensational. Robert Downey Jr.'s portrayal of a black man in *Tropic Thunder* straddles the line, because his makeup is not very dark like traditional blackface. However, his behavior and speech could be seen by many to be very stereotypical. Since he was actually tasteful and funny in the film, he received a general pass from most people. (I'm not talking about a ghetto pass!)

But let's look at a true example of blackface. In Australia, Harry Connick Jr., appeared on a variety show called "*Hey Hey it's Saturday*". This show is a direct ripoff of the Gong Show. Harry became offended when a group calling themselves the "Jackson Jive" started to parody and mimic the Jackson Five in blackface. The makeup was very crude and cartoonish. They had big nappy Afro's. There was no attempt to look like normal black people. The very name Jackson Jive was stereotypical, and put people in the wrong frame of mind. I remember Ted Danson and Whoopi Goldberg being heavily criticized for engaging in a blackface skit. I also remember an episode on TV's *Gimmie a Break*, where little Joey performed in blackface, and offended the main character Nel Carter. As far as I know, blackface is still socially unacceptable. It doesn't matter if Tyra Banks features beautiful models in blackface, or socially thought-provoking director Spike Lee features it in his movie *Bamboozled*. It could even be C. Thomas Howell in the affirmative action bashing movie *Soulman*. Blackface will always strike an uneasy nerve in many people, due to its damaging history.

It's not just white people putting on black makeup to make fun of black people, you also have comedians like Eddie Murphy (SNL), Dave Chapelle, and the Wayans brothers (*White Chicks*), who put on whiteface to make fun of white people. But the modern day minstrel show that black people should be concerned with, comes from black people themselves. After years of fighting to improve the image of the black community, we have rappers and like-minded individuals, clowning and acting like buffoons on rap videos and ethnic themed programming. To me, this is the worst form of blackface! The examples are too numerous to list, but everyone knows the type of behavior that can be summed up in these descriptive words: buffoonery, boorish, ill bred, uncouth, uncultured, uncivilized, unrefined, unpolished, churlish, shuckin and jivin, weak minded, witless, senseless, silly, asinine, brainless, idiotic, moronic, feeble-minded, half cocked, irrational, slow, non intelligent, imbecilic, absurd, goofy, kooky, loony, tomfoolery, wacky, zany, preposterous, dotty, harebrained, dippy, daffy, ridiculous, ludicrous, half-baked, unacceptable, insanity, nonsense, impractical, sappy, nutty, doltish, dimwitted, dumb, dense, simple, block-headed, lamebrain, goosey, numbskulled, pin-headed, foolish, brutish, lumbering, oafish, sluggish, crass, crude, backward, etc.

As black people, we love to have a good time. But as a people, we should never be permanently linked to any of the above words. If any of the above words describe your persona, then you can't be offended by blackface. Don't be a walking stereotype!

Thanks to Siditty.blogspot.com

Stop Snitching—A problem in the black community, but not the Italian community.

If there's one thing that the African-American community and the Italian-American community have in common, it would be its aversion to being a snitch. Being in cahoots with the cops is a no-no in both communities. Hollywood has done its part in reinforcing the "No-Snitch" policy. How many times have you seen a mob movie where a snitch or "rat" is often killed in a very brutal way. Also, movies like A Bronx Tale, have reinforced the rewards for not being a rat. The same theme is interwoven into many black movies featuring the so-called "hood mentality". It should be obvious to most people that the no-snitch policy only benefits criminals, both black and Italian. But the question that seems to linger in my mind is, why is the Italian community not as crippled by the no-snitch policy as the black community?

The black community is not in the same position as the Italian community. For example, when you think of the stereotypical petty criminal, you don't usually think of an Italian man. When you think of a drug dealer, you usually don't think of an Italian man. When you think of a pimp, well you get the picture! To take it a step further, most people don't have as much respect for African-American criminals as they do for Italian mobsters. People tend to think of many Italian mobsters as savvy businessmen who outsmart and sometimes even control law enforcement and political officials. That's why you see many African-American criminals who want to emulate Italian mobsters.

It seems that people in the Italian community have marginalized mobsters. These mafia guys have been relegated to the back and not the front. Sure people may love to see mob movies, but most Italians know that they are only a small segment of the Italian community. In fact, their shine has lost a lot of luster. Unfortunately, this has not been the case in the black community. In fact, with hip-hop sensationalizing the no-snitch policy, it has done tremendous damage to the African-American community, more so than any other community. Many people remember the famous interview between CNN and the rapper Cameron. Cameron said that if a mass murderer were living next door to him, he would not alert the authorities. He said that he would just move somewhere else rather than cooperate with the police. Sadly, that is how too many think in the black community. This way of thinking has led to the loss of many lives. Because if you allow a killer to go free, chances are, they will kill again. So in the final analysis, the only winners of the no-snitch policy are those criminals who exploit the loyalties of the community. The losers, well I'm sure by now you've figured that out.

Lost in Translation

Sometimes we misapply being mistreated or rebuffed. We may think people are doing this because of our race, but it may be because of class distinctions. For example, let's just say that I am out at an eating establishment in Columbia County (Georgia), Soho (New York City), or any other trendy upwardly mobile part of the world. I rushed out of the house so I am not dressed to impress, in fact, I am dressed rather shabby or unkempt. As an African-American male, I can feel many eyes burning straight through me as I sit down to partake in my meal. The majority of these eyes belong to Caucasians. Do I assume that white people are treating me badly because I'm black, or because I look like I belong on the other side of town? If I was dressed in an Armani designer suit, would the same people look upon me with disdain? As African-Americans, it's easy to be extra sensitive when it comes to race. Those of us from the current generation have heard many stories of respectable African-Americans being discriminated against regardless of their dress and grooming. However, many modern African-Americans are free to go into many places that they were formerly forbidden to enter. When we do gain access to these places, many people there may not be used to us being there. But, is this an issue that revolves around the socioeconomic situations of many African-Americans? We tend to want to be in places that will accept us as we are. Not many people are willing to change who they are, to be allowed access to certain places. (And rightly so!) Just keep in mind, that we are not only divided by race in the United States or elsewhere for that matter, but also by class, culture, and other seemingly insignificant factors.

In my opinion, looking down on someone because they are different in any way is bad, no matter the reason. However, when you accuse people of looking down on you because of your race, it carries more weight because of the history of racism in the United States. So if you want to just cast a light on unfair treatment and the reasons aren't cut and dry, don't start with race. It could be just another racial dead end.

If I walked into a fancy eating establishment looking like this, would they look at me funny because I'm Black?

Is Negativity King (At least when it comes to movies)?

In Plain Talk Vol. One, I called the media out for engaging in what I called "Piling It On" when it comes to stories about celebrities of color. This led me to think about some other ways that the media have not only embraced negativity when it comes to black culture, but it almost seems as if the negative behavior of black people becomes critically acclaimed. We all know that society and Hollywood have come a long way from the days of the past when the only roles for people of color were maids, butler's, and uneducated buffoons. When you look on TV today you may see some black shows that cater to stereotypes, but you also see a wide range of roles for people of color. (Presidents, doctors, lawyers, etc.) With that being said, when it comes to the most prestigious awards for movies, which black roles receive the most attention? To be more specific, when it comes to the Academy Awards or Oscars, what has been the recent trend as far as black actors and actresses?

As soon as I asked that question two blurry examples come to people's minds. The first black actor to win an Oscar for best male leading role is Denzel Washington. The only black actress to win an Oscar for best female leading role is Halle Berry. Much attention is given to the two roles that were portrayed by these two individuals. Denzel Washington portrayed a corrupt and crooked cop in the movie Training Day, for which he won his Oscar. Halle Berry's role in the movie Monster's Ball involved an extremely explicit sex scene, but nevertheless she still won an Oscar for her role. It is interesting to note that Angela Bassett was offered this same role but turned it down when she learned that she would be doing a very explicit sex scene. Don't get me wrong, many in the black community were delighted that these two African-Americans received their Oscars. What raised many eyebrows, was their many other roles that they did not get an Oscar for. They received an Oscar for work that was not their best, in many people's eyes. Denzel Washington's portrayal of Malcolm X, was a sight to behold on the silver screen. Many thought that Denzel Washington would have received an Oscar for his portrayal of the "Hurricane" Rubin Carter (famous boxer). Instead he received an Oscar for a very negative character, a crooked cop in Training Day. Once Jamie Foxx received an Oscar for his role as Ray Charles, the controversy started to die down about negative aspects of black culture being celebrated in Hollywood. That was until the movie Precious, based on the novel Push by Sapphire. So now the debate is back on again.

Living in Spanglish—by Ed Morales

While writing Plain Talk Volume One, I began to wonder what views other races had towards racism. Not just white and black, but Asian, Hispanic/Latino, Arabic, etc. The first perspective that I wanted to explore is the

Latino/Hispanic perspective on race and stereotypes. A valuable resource for doing so is the book, Living in Spanglish.

I began to discover that the Spanglish culture has some of the same complaints and concerns that the black community has. For starters, they have issues with light skinned and dark skinned Latinos/Hispanics. Sammy Sosa's drastic appearance brought mainstream media attention to this dilemma. Also, just like the Black/African-American/Negro/Colored controversy, Hispanics/Latinos also have a dispute about what to call themselves as well. Is it Latino, Hispanic, or just sticking to your nationality (Colombian, Peruvian, Puerto Rican, etc.) Ed Morales chooses the term Spanglish, because he feels that describing the mixed language is the best metaphor for a diverse mixed race people. After all, you have all Latinos and Hispanics speaking Spanish, but they are living in an English dominated hemisphere. Many times, the true culture of Spanglish is a assimilation without complete loss of identity. Spanglish is unique to the Americas (North, South, and Central). In many ways, African-Americans have had to go through the same process, although in different ways because of slavery.

Another interesting complaint which is similar to the black community is the negative stereotypical portrayal of Latinos and Hispanics, especially in Hollywood. A common complaint is when non-Latinos or Hispanics play the parts of Latinos and Hispanics in major movies. Examples of this go all the way back to the Westside story, where non-Latino/Hispanics played the major roles. Another famous example is Al Pacino, who played Tony Montana, a Cuban criminal in Scarface. Al Pacino also played Carlito, a Puerto Rican, in Carlito's Way. Lou Diamond Phillips, who is Filipino, played the famous Latino musician Richie Valens in the film La Bamba. Ed Morales calls this situation "the last blackface". This is an obvious reference to the days when white men played the role of black men in minstrel shows by artificially darkening their skin. The analogy also works, because of the negative stereotypical portrayals of Hispanic and Latinos in many of Hollywood's movies.

As the Spanglish community becomes more of a force in the cultural landscape of American life, it will be interesting to see who has the greatest impact. Will the mainstream American culture mold or water down the Spanglish culture, or will the Spanglish culture forever change the dynamics of American politics, race relations, psyche, and all other things related to what we now know as Americana. Only time will tell.

Sammy Sosa—Say it ain't so!

Samuel Peralta Sosa is actually one of my favorite baseball players. I became endeared to him when he was involved in the home run chase with Mark Maguire and in 1997-1998 baseball season. His cheerful demeanor and great sportsmanship earned him a legion of fans. With all that being said, when news broke that Sammy Sosa was trying to be like Michael Jackson, my curiosity was definitely aroused. When I saw the photos, my first reaction was: "say it ain't so Sosa!" Then my next reaction was: "Sammy, you got some explaining to do!" (Imagine me saying this in my worst Ricky Ricardo impersonation voice) Sammy was photographed at the Latin Grammy awards (11/4/09) in Las Vegas with his wife Sonia. Sammy later explained in an interview that his skin was lightened by a skin cream that he was using to soften his skin. He also said the bright lights made him appear lighter in the photograph than he actually was. Not many people were buying this excuse. When Sammy appeared on TV for his interview, you could see a dramatic change in his skin. People began speculating on one of two things about Sammy's skin condition. One, he must have bleached his skin. Two, his skin must have changed because of steroid use. I had a hard time reconciling Sosa's changing his skin on purpose. He seemed to be a handsome man with a nice-looking wife. Now his skin looked lifeless and pale. This must have been some sort of accident. I remember being told by someone that only in America did people obsess over skin color. I was told that Latin America embraces people of all colors. Look at Cuba, Puerto Rico, and Sosa's home country of the Dominican Republic. Surely Sosa does not feel any pressure to change his skin to a lighter color to fit in, does he? I decided that I needed to explore the Latin American culture further, and see if they have the same hangups about skin color that the United States has.

I came across a book, Living in Spanglish, by Ed Morales. This book was written in 2002, but it contains passages that seem prophetic when applied to Sammy Sosa's situation. This is what Ed Morales writes:

> "During their reign as conquerors of Latin America, the Spanish referred to the child of an African and a European as a mulatto, a mule-ly being; it was a branding that made it almost impossible for someone to elevate their social status, except through intermarriage with a lighter skinned partner. For centuries, many Latin Americans had been on a dreary quest to lighten the skin, better the race, mejorar la raza, to achieve social status".

I am not accusing Sammy Sosa of hating his brown skin. I am not accusing him of marrying a lighter skinned wife to "mejorar la raza". All I am saying is that when you add everything up, and you look at Sosa's appearance now compared with the past, you can see why many people are concerned. Sosa's hair is no longer curly, it's very straight. Sosa now wears contacts that lighten the color of his eyes. Many kids look up to Sammy Sosa, I just hope they don't get the wrong idea.

CHAPTER THREE

Racial Book Review

When I wrote Plain Talk Volume 1, I wanted it to be a fresh perspective on the issue of race. So therefore, I did not read many books on race during my writing process. With Plain Talk Volume 2, I decided to go in a different direction. Since we are digging a little deeper this time, I felt that it would be beneficial to read as many books on race that I could to get a cosmopolitan view of what others were thinking. As a service to the reader I have compiled a series of book reviews, so that you can flesh out the good from the bad. This process also gives you insight to some of the writings that have shaped my thoughts as I compose Plain Talk Volume 2. Because whether we are conscious of it or not, the books we read contribute to our opinions on matters. So please enjoy my review/analysis of the following books pertaining to race and other related matters.

Stupid Black Men (How to play the Race Card and Lose)— by Larry Elder

If you let it, the title will throw you off. I must give it to Mr. Elder, although we may not see eye to eye on many issues, he does make some good points about taking responsibility and not letting racism affect your ability to better yourself. My biggest problem with Mr. Elder is that sometimes he comes off as an extreme apologist for issues of race that cannot be defended. For example, if there is a situation involving police brutality, he is very quick to take the side of the police, giving them the benefit of the doubt. Even in situations where there is clearly police brutality, Mr. Elder is prone to make excuses, like citing fatigue or irritability. He uses a monolithic argument to downplay incidences of racial discrimination. He only cites examples that support his side of the argument, thus leaving out the other examples that refute his argument. His position and arguments would be more effective if he were to acknowledge the opposition without belittling them.

***Nigger*—by Randall Kennedy**

Mr. Kennedy provides an honest amount of detailed examples of how the N-word has been used to put people of color down. The use of the N-word in the past was very cavalier. Even in very professional settings, black people were called the N-word. Judges, presidents, and other prominent white people frequently used the N-word in public with impunity. The history of the N-word is a very ugly one. Anyone of any color who still thinks it's okay to use the N-word should definitely read this book. (Hint, Hint: John Mayer, Michael Richards, 50 cent, Chris Rock, etc.)

***Racism (opposing viewpoints)*—by various authors**

This book shows the two sides of many viewpoints on race. Some would say that racism is overblown, and others would disagree. Those who say that racism is overblown would use the argument that many incidents are not indicative of society as a whole. I would happen to disagree. This book also shows how racism affects Asians, Hispanics, Native Americans, African-Americans, etc. One of the controversial issues that this book tackles is affirmative action. It asked the questions, does affirmative action create a feeling of inferiority in minorities? Is affirmative action needed to level the playing field? Is there a such thing as black bigotry or black racism? This book tends to use a lot of statistics to prove their point in order to classify people. One of the reasons I tend to shy away from statistics is because they can be manipulated to serve anyone's purpose. If you don't believe me, then take a criminal justice class at your local university.

***Think about Racism*—by Linda Mizell**

This book traces the history of racism and how people have used race as an excuse to treat people as less than human. Slavery has always been a part of human history. For the first time, race was used to justify slavery when Africans were enslaved. Up until that point, most people took slaves as a byproduct of war. According to this book, the so-called Christians of Europe needed a reason to justify owning other human beings. So they came up with the inferiority of someone based on the color of their skin. So it seems the manufactured notion of race was now used to justify treating slaves like property.

The Native Americans were treated poorly before the African slaves in the United States. They were systematically eliminated from prominence. The tactics used by the United States government range from trickery (going back on treaties with Native Americans) to outright massacre (Wounded Knee). The history of the United States is one of institutionalized racism. In order for the status quo to be successful, minorities had to be exploited. When it seemed like they were making inroads, that's when the discrimination and violence would be turned up a notch.

Culture of Intolerance—by Mark Nathan Cohen

Mr. Cohen makes the strong and convincing case that there is no such thing as race. He uses anthropology and genetics to show the complexity of the human family. For example: Southern India—dark skin/ Africans—dark skin/ Aborigines (Australia)—dark skin. Yet these groups cannot be classified into any particular race. When people in the United States refer to race, they are really talking about culture and class. Race was talked up by European philosophers to justify Manifest Destiny and global conquest. Race was used to commit genocide against the Native Americans and the brutal enslavement of Africans, as well as Jim Crow and every other institutional form of racism and discrimination against all non-Anglo races.

Many minorities in the United States have known for long periods of time that the functions of trials in the United States is not always about guilt or innocence. It is rather about latent functions, maintenance of order, reinforcement of group values, symbolic punishment, prejudice and hate, etc.

This book also examines a well-known book called *The Bell Curve*: Intelligence and Class Structure in American Life (1994) by Richard J. Herrnstein and Charles Murray. The Bell Curve tries to prove that people are in poverty or are oppressed because of genetics. This book also makes a scapegoat out of the poor and minorities, who are probably not going to read this book and thus, cannot even defend themselves. The authors heavily rely on IQ tests to prove their points, which is suspect in itself. I once wrote an essay in college that looked at the validity of IQ tests and SAT scores to prove intelligence. The main two problems that I have with tests like these are that they are heavily biased when it comes to cultural vocabulary and hidden cultural assumptions. We know of many examples of people who are very poor, who are taken out of that environment and put in an environment where they can flourish. Right here in Augusta, we had an example of a young man who came from government housing to being admitted at an Ivy League college. All over the world there are stories of people who refuse to be defined by mere tests and socioeconomic confines.

This book addresses something that I brought out in Plain Talk Volume One:*(The Angry White Male)* The angry white male's anger with the state of the world is peculiar, seeing as how they have come from a status of high privilege and access, to one of slightly less privileged. At worst, they are on a level playing field with everyone else. Where was their frustration and sense of justice and fair play when minorities and women were marginalized, frustrated, and discriminated against. It seems disingenuous for the angry white male to be causing an uproar now. Such anger has always been the case in American history when it was perceived that a minority group was "getting ahead". One thing that we have to do as a society is to watch for scapegoats. People often use them to distract your attention from the "real" or "fundamental" issues or causes of problems.

Is Racism a Serious Problem? (At issue—social issues)
by various authors

One of the authors in this book, Shelby Steele, makes the case of the perception of racism being more powerful and harmful than actual racism. He claims that white supremacy is defeated. He also says that whites can't get away with the things they used to do. With that being said, he says that blacks need to break out of the victim mentality. This is a common thread among the thoughts of many black conservatives. To rebut his claims, many people would bring up the Jena 6 situation or Hurricane Katrina as examples that actual racism is quite harmful.

***A Country of Strangers*—by David K. Shipler**

This book brings out an interesting array of issues, one being black biculturalism, or code switching. Is it okay to code switch? Is it really necessary? Those who are black and work in professional environments know the answer to those questions.

This book brings out some interesting points on the Thomas Jefferson and Sally Hemmings relationship. For those who don't know, former president of the United States, Thomas Jefferson, was said to be in a relationship with a former slave, Sally Hemmings. What's so interesting is that Thomas Jefferson wrote about many of the stereotypes of blacks. Stereotypes such as being mentally inferior, lazy, etc. Unfortunately, Mr. Jefferson did not account for the institution of slavery as being a factor. He even went so far as to say that black people smell differently. Was this how Mr. Jefferson really felt, or was he throwing up a smokescreen to mask his true feelings for black people.

Benjamin Banneker, the brilliant surveyor and astronomer who helped lay out Washington DC, called out Thomas Jefferson. In so many words, Mr. Banneker said: how could you be so vigilant in fighting to get out of the yoke of the British crown, and then turn around and become the very thing you fought against by supporting the oppression of black people. Mr. Banneker also accused Thomas Jefferson of being contrary to Almighty God by supporting slavery. This whole situation reminds me of Sen. Strom Thurmond, who for many years was a staunch supporter of segregation. Only later in life did we find out that he had a relationship with a black woman, which led to him fathering a daughter. Or think about politician Mark Foley, who spoke out against the homosexual lifestyle, only to find out later that he was a homosexual.

Artist Grady Abrams imagines through his art, what Strom Thurmond and his daughter Essie Mae would have looked like, if they were not worried about what society would have thought of their relationship. (Strom secretly cared for Essie Mae financially.)

He Talk Like a White Boy—by Joseph C. Phillips

Mr. Phillips bears his soul and delivers a complete analysis of what it is like being black and unique. when you hear Mr. Phillips talk, you know he is proud to be black. He is also proud to be an American and refuses to pick one over the other. Although I don't agree with many of his political views, and I also would have never walked that White Girl to the office. (Read the book to find out what I am talking about) I do agree with Mr. Phillips on a core number of issues, mainly the value of a good education and not being a victim. I think more Black people should value people like Mr. Phillips. He is intelligent and represents his family and race in a fine manner. I don't think White people should have the market cornered on proper speech and intelligence. I have to fight with my family members on not thinking with a small mind when it comes to education. Why should kids admire those who are pimping their race for money? Why not admire people like Mr. Phillips who is grounded in many positive attributes? You don't have to agree with a person to admire their qualities. Even though Mr. Phillips is a conservative, he has not adopted the attitude of many conservatives with respect to looking down on those less fortunate than himself. I enjoyed reading this book, because it gives me a fresh perspective and new ways of looking at things.

Losing the Race: Self-Sabotage in Black America—by John H. McWhorter

I have enjoyed reading John McWhorter's books. He is now my new favorite author. He thinks outside of the box. The only major issue that I disagree with him on is the O.J. situation. I don't think that the Prosecution had a slam dunk case, but I digress. Mr. McWhorter hit the nail on the head when he addressed making yourself a victim, the black community's natural aversion to intellectual activity, and separating from mainstream society. (to the point where it hinders your upward mobility) Two things in this book have stuck in my mind. Firstly, I write about people calling things racist, when it may be something else. Mr. McWhorter brought out how some people may not be racist, but they have a "lack of imagination". I have seen this barrier in so many aspects of life. I am grateful to those who have broken barriers. People like Jimi Hendrix, whose artistry knew no boundaries. Secondly, the other thing that stuck in my mind is a part towards the end of the book, where he says we have to switch to the second phase of the Civil Rights movement.

The first phase, was getting a level playing field, now the second phase is actually getting out there and playing!!! Great analogy!!

***Dreams from My Father: A Story of Race and Inheritance*— by Barack Obama**

I envy those who read this book before Obama became president. I also can admit that if he never rose up the ranks, then I would have never heard of this book. The struggles of bi-racial children are often left untold. The conflict in a world that chooses you to pick sides is almost unbearable. Barack tells his story with flair and charm and a sense of aloofness. It is a shame that black fathers tend to not stick with their children in bi-racial relationships. I understand the strain that can cause these conditions, but the abandoned child is often the one bearing the most weight. I have seen many young men who are in Barack's predicament veer off on the wrong path. Thank goodness that he did not. As bi-racial children become more prominent, we may truly understand their lot in life. Hopefully that means not having to pick sides!!

***His Panic: Why Americans Fear Hispanics in The U.S.*— by Geraldo Rivera**

I enjoyed reading Hispanic because I sense a growing tide of angst against many Latinos and Hispanics. If you look Mexican, many times you are assumed to be here illegally. One thing all should agree with is that Immigration needs to be fixed. It is unrealistic to think that we could round up all illegals and send them out of the country. Mexicans are not the only ones here illegally. You have many Europeans that have over stayed their Visas. They benefit from their resemblance to mainstream America. You also have many Africans who are here illegally. We need to get everyone on the books and have them paying taxes immediately. Think of the time and money it would take to round up all illegals. People don't even want to pay for Health Care or Quality Education. The only part of the book that I took offense to is the sugarcoating of Fox's coverage of the Immigration debate. (Geraldo works for Fox News) How do you think they get their ratings? CNN just had Lou Dobbs pushing the extremist agenda and now he no longer works for CNN. I even included Lou Dobbs in my first volume of Plain Talk. I talked about the time when he almost had a slip up with Condelezza Rice. (cotton picker—quickly changed to cotton picking)

***Race Experts: How Racial Etiquette, Sensitivity Training, and New Age Therapy Hijacked the Civil Rights Revolution*— by Elisabeth Lasch-Quinn**

When looking at the title and liner notes, I thought this book was going to focus on Race Experts that we all know. (Jesse Jackson, Al Sharpton) Or maybe this book will focus on talking heads that we always see on T.V. talking about race—Michael Eric Dyson, Cornel West, Skip Gates, Larry Elder) Instead, most of the book centered on obscure workshops that most people have never heard of. I did enjoy many aspects of the book. My favorite was the discussion of the book Nappy Hair. I vaguely remember this event, but Race Experts made many things clear. If I were the child of an African-American child in 3rd grade, I would not want a white teacher reading a book of that nature to my child. It's amazing that this teacher, being inexperienced, did not consult another teacher before reading Nappy Hair to the class. The parents had a right to be angry, but not that angry. In my book Plain Talk, I state upfront, that I do not believe that there is a such thing as a Race Expert. This book has solidified my stance.

***Living in Spanglish: The Search for Latino Identity in America*— by Ed Morales**

As a fellow writer of books on ethnicity, I became curious of other viewpoints. Since Latinos/Hispanics are a rapidly growing segment of the U.S. population, I felt a responsibility to examine some of the issues in the Latino community. I found many similarities between the Black and Latino communities when it comes to stereotypes and Race. 1. What do we call ourselves? 2. Stereotypical treatment in Hollywood. 3. Light skin vs. dark skin (Sammy Sosa) I just wish the book wasn't so long. I guess those who are interested in obscure history will love those parts. Thanks for opening my eyes to many things Ed Morales!!

***HOW TO DEAL WITH WHITE PEOPLE*—by David Goldberg**

I am the author of a similar book called Plain Talk-Everything you ever and never wanted to know about Racism and Stereotypes. Volume One. I agree with another reviewer who gave note to the brevity of this book. I also believe that when books drag on too long, it takes away from the reader being able to grasp important points. I am a strong proponent of people of all races creating similar books, so that we can understand one another. Now we need books like this from Asians, Hispanics, etc. There were some valid points brought out that may be hard for some to swallow, but people will find fault in the delivery. This book stems from years of white supremacy dominating the face of American culture. White people need to read this book so that they can see how many people of color feel about them. I was shocked to learn that the writer of this book was not David Goldberg, but rather a man named Jela Oba Okpara. You could tell anyway once you start reading the book. I have corresponded with the author several times and he seemed to have good intentions. If you have an open mind and want to find out other people's point of view, then this book will be an interesting read. The most profound statement of the book comes at the end, when the author proclaims: What's the best way to deal with white people, not to deal with them at all! Does David Goldberg/Jela Oba Okpara make a good enough case to make a statement like that? You'll have to read this book and decide for yourself. (I found it interesting that the author said that white people were also a part of the intended audience)

***Plain Talk Vol. 1 (Everything you ever and never wanted to know about racism and stereotypes)*—an Independent review by Simon Barrett**

There is no doubt in my mind that racism is alive and well. It may well be the largest growing 'sport' in the country. I see it everywhere I look, it matters not one iota what your roots are, it only matters where you find yourself. Sometimes racism merely is an annoyance, as in being asked something like you are not from around here?

On other occasions it takes a much more sinister turn. One only has to look at the past to understand the present, and it is easy to make assumptions about the future.

Corey Washington pulls no punches, he takes racism head on. It is wrong, it should not exist, racism should be a class taught in history classes, not something that we deal with today. Yet it is a subject that we hear about on a daily basis. There are also many double standards as to what can, or can not be said. Maybe the biggest issue in the US is the use of the `N' word. It is happily bandied about in Rap songs, but woe be that any white person should make such a remark. Careers have been ruined by the `N' word.

Corey Washington makes the very convincing argument that no-one should use the word PERIOD. I am in agreement, but the likelihood of that happening is right up there with discovering that the Moon is indeed made of cheese!

The nasty `N' word is just the tip of the iceberg, you can find derogatory descriptions of the doyens of many countries.

I grew up in England and the favorite target was Paddy the not quite intelligent Irishman. During my stay in Germany I found that the favorite target were the Gast Arbeiters (Guest workers), mainly from Poland that were ridiculed.

One common thread that I have found in this subject is that the stories stay the same, only the races involved change.

Corey Washington takes us into the very murky world of racism and stereotyping. I thought I had a pretty large vocabulary of disparaging remarks, but Corey Washington has me beat, he has researched the subject more than I ever would have.

I think this sentiment comes out best in the opening paragraph:

> I'm not an expert on race. Well, nobody is. Don't let any of these TV pundits or anyone else fool you—nobody has a hold on the title of "race expert." Now there are people who have spent a great deal of time studying and compiling data on race, and people who have spent a great deal of time interviewing people and getting their experiences and thoughts down for the record; but that doesn't make anyone an expert. The truth of the matter is everyone's experience with racism is different. All we can do is open an honest and sincere dialogue to learn from one another.

It is easy to stick labels on people. This is a game that we all have played for centuries. Without doubt the new label involves anyone that is a Muslim, they must be a terrorist! In fact the quote goes along the lines of:

> Not all Muslims are terrorists, but all terrorists are Muslims.

While the statement rings true in many ears, it is completely wrong. The Baader Meinhoff group were certainly not Muslim. Neither were the Japanese sect that released Sarin gas into the subway system.

Time is very much a double edged sword. And few people have long memories. If you look back in history it is plain to see that racism is wrong, yet we ignore that and let it flourish in our modern world. Do not get me wrong I am not asking that we take this to the ridiculous lengths of Political

Correctness that some might advocate, just that we show a little common courtesy. I am a white Caucasian who happens to live in a predominantly African American neighborhood. When outside the most common swearword I hear is the `N' word. It is not the white Caucasians that I hear it from but the African Americans, particularly the young teens. The word is used as a term of endearment!

I found Plain Talk to be a very challenging book, oh, do not get me wrong, when I say challenging I am not talking about the quality of the writing, it is first rate. It is the subject matter that gives me concern. I will pose the question, how do we remove racism from today's world?

Plain Talk has had me sleepless for days. You can pick up your copy from Amazon. Corey Washington also has a web site in support of the book.

Simon Barrett

Race Matters—by Cornel West

One of the first things that you notice about the book-Race Matters by Cornel West is the length, or lack thereof. However when you read Race Matters, you realize why Dr. West chooses to make it short and sweet. Does this book need to be updated now that we have an Afr.-Amer. president? Unfortunately, no! I would like to see Dr. West create a Race Matters Vol. 2. Dr. West is not a monolithic Afr.-Amer. author/thinker. He had no problem supporting Obama for the Pres., but when he sees Obama not sticking up for the downtrodden, he's ready to offer constructive criticism.

How to Make Black America Better: Leading African Americans Speak Out— by Tavis Smiley

I saw Tavis Smiley's name, but I did not read much from him in the book. I should have saw where it said compiled and edited by Tavis Smiley. I enjoyed the two sessions with the panels at the end of the book. I also enjoyed the various essays by some of the celebrities. I am worried that the black community is looking for leaders instead of being one themselves. I want to hear what ordinary people have to say about making Black America better. Shaq's ideas about the improvement of Black America are not more important than a janitor at your local high school, yet we hear Shaq's opinion more than the regular folks. That's not to slight Shaq in anyway. In fact, he's one of my favorite B-Ball players. I just felt that many of the celebrities featured in the book had nothing of substance to add to the conversation. They were only included in the book because they were famous.

***Is Bill Cosby Right?: Or Has the Black Middle Class Lost Its Mind?*—by Michael Eric Dyson**

As soon as I saw the title, I knew that this was a book that I wanted to read. It did not disappoint! MED puts forth his points in an intelligent sympathetic way to disable those who would charge him of being a hater. I especially enjoyed the point about the images of the Fat Albert gang and how it relates to the images of those who Cosby now condemns. I just heard Mr. Cosby give an interview on Sirius Sat. radio where he explains that he just got tired of saying the same thing over again. He wanted to put a little fire behind his message. Looks like Mr. Cosby was very effective in doing so . . . he got MED to write a whole book about his tirade. I see both sides of the argument. To Mr. Cosby's credit he has devoted a great deal of time to opening dialogue amongst young and old and everyone in between. Thanks Cos and MED!

***Race Rules: Navigating the Color Line*—by Michael Eric Dyson**

As the author of a new series on Race called Plain Talk, I decided to read as many books that I could before writing Vol. 2 of Plain Talk. One of the books that I brought was Race Rules. I had favorites and not so favorites in this book. Some may not be interested in the million man march or the dynamics of the lack of feminist influence on the march. However, you may be interested in MED's introspective rendering of the inner sanctum of the pastor's circle. I won't give it away, but MED bares his soul. I also enjoyed the discussion on O.J. and what it said about our society. In my book Plain Talk, I also examine the polarizing aspects of this whole episode, as well as many other events. There is something for everyone in Race Rules.

***What do White Americans Want to Know about Black Americans but are Afraid to Ask*—by John H. Davis**

I was very interested to read what Mr. Davis had to say about matters of race. This is the sort of book that seems written for White Americans, but all can benefit. It is informative to know others views on your race as a whole. You may disagree with some points, but there are a lot of points that will make you think. That's the most important part. He makes some poignant observations about the things that he has seen with his own eyes. Also research is provided to back up certain arguments. This book will keep your interest until the very end. As soon as you look at the table of contents, you will be hooked. As a fellow author of a book on Racism, I highly recommend this book for all races.

Authentically Black—by John H. McWhorter

John McWhorter has one common theme throughout all of his books—don't put him in a box! Some Liberals will agree with some things, some conservatives will agree. The same goes with various races. Ultimately, I agree with the main theme of taking responsibility and not making excuses for the many shortcomings of the way things were and are. Some areas where we disagree would be his assessment of progress. For example, Mr. McWhorter makes the statement that "most blacks are not poor." I disagree, because you have to actually define poor. Most of us can go to any major city and go to the worst part of town and see what the majority of the poorest people's skin color is. You don't need someone to do a fancy-schmancy study to figure that one out. It is a given, that year over year, black unemployment is always higher than other groups. The only group that is higher would be teenagers. Anytime you use polls and statistics to support your claims, you are treading on thin ice. You have to ask yourself: Who did these people actually poll? You can always fudge facts in order to prove a point. This was a sobering point that I learned in criminology class at Augusta State University. But for anyone that has actually lived in New York's housing projects, or any other impoverished area of the world, reality stares you in the face every day of your life.

I am not for a "victim mentality" type of attitude. I know that this way of thinking is a waste of time and energy. I am definitely not for "blaming the white man." I just don't want to go above and beyond trying to sugarcoat reality. I see race becoming a growing problem due to the dynamics of the racial make up in this country. What happens when many figure out that there are more people of color then they thought. Someone needs to write a book about that. The title Authentically Black is very provocative because, who decides who's black and who's not? As the definition of black expands, then so will the possibilities.

It's not all doom and gloom when it comes to racial progression. Let's just look at one segment, portrayal of minorities on TV, in order to prove a point. If you were to look at the situation in the 1950s and compare it with the situation today, you would find pros and cons. It's like a double-edged sword, so to speak. On the pro side, today you would see minorities in a wide variety of roles. Roles such as doctors, lawyers, teachers, even presidents and CEO's. You have many roles where minorities are cast into intelligent characters that show tremendous depth. And we are not just talking about menial characters, but actual leading roles. Shows like The Unit, and a host of other crime dramas come to mind. On the con side, you have a great deal of shows that lean toward the stereotypical side. These shows often show minorities engaging in and embarrassing behaviors, all for a laugh. Although in all fairness, many of those so-called "lowbrow" shows, while showing some minstrel-like buffoonery, also sometimes show characters who are sensitive and sensible. These points that I have mused on are only the tip of the iceberg when it comes to talking points in Authentically Black. I suggest you pick it up for yourself for further discussion.

***Race and Ethnicity in America (A Concise History)—* Ronald H. Bayor-Editor**

In the past, many African-Americans have had to wear the mask of racial submission. In other words, if you wanted to keep your job, or life, you have to have a certain demeanor. This led to the stereotype of black people being happy-go-lucky. That's why it seemed that they always had a smile on their face.

As you study the history of discrimination and racial violence, you see that African-Americans aren't the only ones subjected to these vices. We know about the depletion of the Native Americans, but you also have the vicious mob violence against the Chinese workers in the Western United States. Also, Mexicans are constantly being harassed in the United States regardless of their immigration status. Who knows, they could even be a Hispanic American whose ancestors were here before Europeans. Or they could be Puerto Ricans, who are natural citizens of the United States. Lastly, they could be Mexicans who are here legally with a valid work visa. That is why immigration reform needs to be handled with care.

Many people don't think of the discrimination of the Irish, Italians, etc. because these groups are often considered white. The reason that African-American discrimination and related topics trump all of these other races has to do with the issue of slavery. The question is: what is it going to take for the two sides to come to some kind of agreement? Should the goal be to come to an agreement? Maybe the word understanding should be substituted for agreement. If there is going to be more of an agreement reached on race, society needs to stop considering the subject of race controversial. Is it really the actual subject of race, or how people deal with racial issues that generates so much controversy? I believe it to be the latter! The goal should be to frame a new way of talking about race that takes into account the many pitfalls of the past discussions on race. People need to be briefed right up front, that some things will be said that may hurt or offend you, but it should be your job to try to understand where the other person is coming from and also to correct any inaccuracies or false and misguided information. I'm not naïve. I know that some people choose to be ignorant, and it would be a waste of time to discuss anything of substance with them. This method is only for those who sincerely want to understand other races or cultures.

CHAPTER FOUR

People Places and Things (Points of Racial Discussion)

(The first four segments are New York related) Attica Prison Riot—September 1971

A prison riot broke out among the inmates at Attica prison, which is near Buffalo, New York. Most of the inmates were black and all of the guards were white. Prisoners were protesting what they felt were horrible conditions that included racism. The prisoners seized hostages, blindfolded them, and threaten to slash their throats. When negotiations broke down, hostages were marched outside in full view of television cameras. All of a sudden, teargas was dropped in a commando style raid, which resulted in the deaths of 29 inmates. Nine of the hostages were also killed. Word soon spread that the prisoners had killed the dead guards by slashing their throats. Other rumors included one guard being castrated, and other guards being severely stabbed in the intestines. Although these accounts seemed credible because of the built in stereotype of the violent and vicious brute, known as the black male criminal. It was soon revealed by autopsy that the nine hostages did not die by the prisoners hand's, but rather the bullets of the all white police assault team.

This story would not even be worth mentioning, but the majority of the people in the town of Attica could not believe that the protective hand of the police would kill one of their own. We now know from various wars that this is called "friendly fire." Many in the community had a set mental belief that demanded that the killers be the brutal black prisoners. This goes back to what I said about perception becoming reality in PT Vol. 1. Many black people could easily believe that the police would sacrifice their own to take down a prison riot. Past experiences in their minds no doubt influenced their perceptions. However, many whites, just like in the OJ case, believe in the flawless reputation of law enforcement to always do the right thing. Both communities saw the same event, but their perception of reality and the interpretations of past events was what polarized the opinions of the two races.

This is no accident, these conditions have emerged because of racism being an institution, not only in the United States, but around the world. I know exactly who is behind these conditions, but the answer is a spiritual one and requires the seeker to think on a spiritual plane. Since this is not the focus of this book, I will refrain from going down that path. (Hint: 2 Corinthians 4:4)

The same absolute violent criminal aspirations have been haphazardly cast upon black men throughout the history of the United States. As I touched on briefly in Plain Talk volume 1, the case of Susan Smith brings this to the fore. This is the case where she accused a black man of carjacking her and kidnapping her two kids. It was not hard for the media and the white community to believe Susan Smith. I also touched on the case of Carol and Charles Stewart from Boston. This is the case where Charles Stewart called 911 with a phony story of a black man killing his pregnant wife. Immediately this imaginary black man was sought, thus castigating or punishing the Roxbury community of Boston. Unlike the Susan Smith case, where no black males were arrested, the Boston Police Department pressured Dereck Jackson, a 17-year-old boy, to falsely accuse William Bennett. In a dastardly deed, Charles Stewart identified Mr. Bennett as the killer, which subsequently led to Mr. Bennett's arrest. If it wasn't for Charles Stewart's brother Matthew Stewart coming clean about his brothers elaborate hoax to kill his wife to collect a life insurance payment, Mr. Bennett may still be rotting in jail. Charles Stewart felt the screws tightening around him, so he did the cowardly thing and took his own life by jumping off a bridge.

Even though we are mainly talking about the stereotypical role of the black male as a criminal, sometimes this extends to Hispanics as well. Case in point, Jennifer Wilbanks, also known as the runaway bride, falsely told her fiancé that a Hispanic man had kidnapped and sexually assaulted her. Once again, the media sensationalized her story and ran with it. Since she was calling from Albuquerque, New Mexico, it probably seemed logical from her standpoint to use a Hispanic male, rather than a black male.

Since the Plain Talk series is not one-sided, sometimes black people have capitalized off of the stereotype of whites being racist. Just look at the Tawanna Brawley case and the Duke lacrosse case. Both women used the stereotype of the white male taking liberties with black women. We know that this was a common occurrence in the slavery days, but these two women used the past to gain the sympathy of the black community. So that proves my point even further. Whites and blacks sometimes use racial stereotypes to their own advantage. The only way to lessen the chance at doing this kind of foolishness, is to properly educate people on stereotypes. That is one of many objectives of the Plain Talk series.

Howard Beach, NYC (Dec. 20th 1986)

A trademark of gangs is to protect their turf. They don't want any outsiders coming into their neighborhood. Is it any different when some overzealous neighborhoods do the same thing based on the color of someone's skin? No! The Howard Beach incident bore this out:

Even though New York City is one of the most diverse cities in the world, there are still ethnic enclaves that silently keep their neighborhood exclusively white. Many people within the city just know to stay out of certain places. I used to live in Marlboro Homes (projects) in the Gravesend /Bensonhurst area of Brooklyn. I know firsthand the imaginary walls of segregation that exist in New York City. I remember having to walk through all white neighborhoods to get to PS (Public school) 95. I remember being threatened by older whites on at least two occasions. One time, two whites, while driving on a moped, threw some iced tea on me. I may have said something to cause them to circle back, but nothing really happened. On another occasion, I was walking through a path going to school and was threatened by two older white kids. One said to the other: "Let's leave him alone, he's too young". This all happened in 1984-85, right before New York City turned into a racial powder keg. I was only eight or nine at the time.

On December 20, 1986, three black men were driving through Howard Beach, until their car broke down. When some neighborhood people saw them, they let them know through racial epithets, that they were not welcome. But since they were hungry, they decided to stick around and eat at a local pizza parlor. When they got ready to leave, they were greeted by a mob of angry whites with baseball bats. As you can imagine, what happened next was not pretty. The three men were pummeled and started to flee. One of the black men, 23-year-old Michael Griffin, ran into the street and was struck and killed by car.

The incident drew national attention to the segregated Howard Beach area, because at the time, people were putting pressure on South Africa to end apartheid. How ironic was it that New York City had a similar apartheid situation. Many in the media started comparing Howard Beach to the old South. It is also ironic that the actions of the white mob to keep three black men out of their neighborhood, led to many black protesters showing up in their neighborhood to protest.

As the trial ensued, the lawyers for the defense dug up as much dirt on the deceased and surviving two black plaintiffs, in an effort to deflect from the aggression of the white mob. It was obvious that these two guys were not poster children for model citizens. But what did all of that have to do with the crimes that were committed by the mob of angry whites? Absolutely nothing, so the jury convicted three out of the four defendants.

Lessons: there probably were harsh words thrown in both directions from both white and black people, but the bottom line is: violence only leads to death or trouble when it comes to race. Today, those men may have been charged with a hate crime. Looking back, those three black guys should have went back into the pizza parlor and asked the manager to call the police. At the very least, they should have locked themselves in a bathroom. Don't try to be a hero! (It was discovered later on that one of the men brandished a knife.) With all that being said, was it worth it to keep people who look different than you out of your neighborhood. These black men were going to leave soon enough. Like the Beatles sang: Let it be!

Source: www.queentribute.com

Bensonhurst, NYC (August 23rd, 1989)

Yusef Hawkins and three friends came to the predominantly Italian neighborhood of Bensonhurst (Brooklyn) to look for a car. They were met by a mob of 30 white youths who were angry that a white girl invited minorities to her birthday party. One of the white youths had a gun. They thought Yusef and his friends were there for the party, and the situation escalated to the point of Yusef being shot and murdered.

This led to a massive protest in Bensonhurst, in which Rev. Al Sharpton took a pivotal role. The media got to see the hostility of the angry white residents of Bensonhurst, as they chanted "useless", "useless". (A take on Yusef's name) One person even spat in the face of Yusef's father, Moses Stewart. (This reminds me of the incident with the Tea Party protesters and black congressman.)

In 1991, Al Sharpton was stabbed leading a march through Bensonhurst. The attacker later felt remorse and was forgiven by Mr. Sharpton. In 1998, one of the attackers of Yusef Hawkins was released early from prison, which led to more protests. Even today there are still hostilities, but many whites will admit that they don't want to do anything that will bring Al Sharpton back into their neighborhood.

Back when I lived in the Bensonhurst area, I remember going to school with all different races. Even though we all went to the same school with each other, we knew that after school, the Blacks and Puerto Ricans would go back to the projects, and the whites would go to their homes. You could literally count the number of white families in the Marlboro Homes on one hand. The only white family that I knew of was Third World poor, and even I felt sorry for them. It just goes to show you that segregation is not exclusive to the south.

Lesson: see Howard Beach

Source: Jennifer Marino—NYU—Journalism Dept.

Central Park Jogger (Apr. 19th 1989)

Trisha Meili, a 28-year-old investment banker, decided to go for a jog in New York's infamous Central Park. She somehow felt it would be safe jogging alone at night. It was a very costly miscalculation, because she was brutally raped and beaten in one of New York's most brutal and high profile crimes. (That's saying a lot!) That same night that she was brutally assaulted, there were packs of young black and Hispanic teens attacking strangers in Central Park. (Just like the flash mobs that we hear about in Philadelphia) The police came to the stereotypical albeit logical conclusion, that the perpetrators must have come from these gangs of roving teens. The mainly white media in New York put out false information that these youths were engaging in an activity called "wilding". In fact, these young men were repeating the lyrics of a popular rap song at that time by Tone Loc called "Wild Thang".

There were only five youths out of the more than 30 that roamed the park, charged with his brutal crime. All of the youths were ages 14 to 16. They were not from broken ghetto homes, but rather traditional two-parent households. They had no previous criminal record. There was no physical evidence linking them to the crime. The only evidence was taped confessions, which were quickly recanted when they were allowed to be with their lawyers and parents. The youth said they were coerced by the police through either lies, intimidation, or other means. A red flag should have gone up when it was discovered that the youths parents or lawyers were not present during these confessions. Nevertheless, all five were convicted. Unfortunately, numerous rapes and brutal murders occur in New York City with a high rate of frequency. Many in the black community wondered if the climate was ratcheted up because of the race of the victim and the alleged perpetrators.

When going back and looking at the so-called confessions, you find many troubling discrepancies. It's seemed as if the young men were just making things up to get out of a bad situation. The media also joined in the feeding frenzy by promoting a double standard. Most media outlets did not release the name of the Central Park jogger, but saw no need to withhold the names of the juvenile suspects. They even released the name of one boy who was not even charged in the crime. This led to a very divisive racial climate in New York City. Many black media outlets released the name of Trisha Meili as a response to the double standard.

Finally in 2002, Matias Reyes, serving life in prison, confessed to the brutal crime. He said that he acted alone and had no help. DNA confirmed that he was indeed the attacker. But what about the five youths charged of the crime. In a bizarre stand that created even more minority mistrust of the cops, the NYPD still would not admit that the confessions were false and coerced. Finally, on December 19th of 2002, the convictions of the five youths were vacated. The sad part that is not reported on in the media, is that a few months after the real killer confessed, Trisha Meili came out with a book called "I am the Central Park Jogger." I went to her website and it still pretends that these five young men committed this brutal crime. It doesn't even mention the confession of the real perpetrator, Matias Reyes. I e-mailed Mrs. Meili and asked her to update her website to tell the truth. I understand that the book was probably written before the confession, but it would be humane to pull the books and insert the correct information. The very least you could do is update the webpage!

By her own admission, Mrs. Meili has no recollection of the brutal attack that she suffered, so all of the information in her book about the attack came from news reports, which many turned out to be false. The five young men originally convicted never had a run-in with the police. All of a sudden, one day they decide to engage in one of New York's most notorious and vicious crimes. It just doesn't add up! The five young men, now my age, who were falsely accused, have to live with the stigma of being criminals. Even though they were exonerated, there are still many in the white community who stubbornly refuse to admit that the police messed up. This is the kind of situation that causes the black and white community to see high profile criminal cases like: OJ, Rodney King, Susan Smith, and other similar cases in a different light. Once again the media did not help the situation. Even Kobe Bryant is still called a rapist by a white fan every now and then at an NBA game. Wait a minute, I thought it was innocent until proven guilty. But you can also add: If you are falsely proven guilty, it is hard to get your innocence restored if you are a person of color. (Or a teacher of any color accused of a sex crime with a child)

Sources: NY Times/ Daily News/ www.centralparkjogger.com

Virginia Beach—a.k.a. "Greekfest riots" (Labor Day Weekend 1989)

College students descending on resort towns are not uncommon in the United States. Daytona Beach, Florida, Myrtle Beach, South Carolina, and Fort Lauderdale, Florida are popular spots for college kids. But on Labor Day Weekend in 1989, at the Greekfest in Virginia Beach, a riot broke out that many feel was racially motivated.

The story really starts in the years before 1989. City officials claim that the black college themed Greekfest had a bad reputation for leaving the city in shambles. On the other hand, many in the black community charged that the damage from the Greekfest was no different than the damage is less by why colleges. The city finally had enough and made sure that the 1989 Greekfest attendees felt as unwelcome as possible. How the riots started, no one really knows, but many people saw the barricades and heavy police presence and saw a big confrontation coming a mile away. The end result,

500 arrests and very costly property damage. When the dust settled and people were able to figure out what happened, it seemed that most people agreed that a show of police force combined with closing a public beach was enough to send some people over the edge. Unfortunately, many black festival attendees got caught in the crossfire and was on the receiving end of overly aggressive police attention. (A.K.A. police brutality) In the years after the Greekfest riots, the city installed extensive surveillance equipment, thus killing the Greekfest, because nobody wants to be spied on!

Since I live in Georgia, we can definitely relate to the story because of Atlanta's infamous Freaknik. Since its inception in 1982, it grew to some 250,000 people at some point. Many videos showed complete lawlessness and lewd behavior at the Freaknik. Eventually, city officials did the same thing that Virginia Beach did: make attendees as unwelcome as possible. After moving the Freaknik to Daytona Beach, Florida, it eventually died down.

On a smaller scale, these accounts remind me of what would happen to us when we would find a nice court or gym to play basketball at. As long as it was a few people within our inner circle playing, everything was fine. But when people started inviting other people, the experience quickly turned sour. I guess the same could be said for a good fishing hole.

(The next two segments are Georgia related)
Forsyth County GA (Jan. 17th, 1987)

Forsyth County has seemingly always had an ugly racial history, with the most notable being the racial cleansing of 1912. Lynch mobs ruled the day and black citizens were terrorized to the point of fleeing the area. Fast-forward to the 1980s and you had civil rights demonstrations, and counter demonstrations by Ku Klux Klan members. On January 17, 1987, violence ensued which led to the injuries of civil rights marchers and the arrests of eight counter-demonstrators. A week later, 20,000 civil rights marchers demonstrated in Cumming, Georgia, compared with 5,000-6000 counter-demonstrators. This was the largest civil rights demonstration in the United States since 1970. Due to a large and costly ($670,000) police presence, no violence took place, despite the huge number of participants. All of this spawned from an attempt to show the world that Forsyth County, Georgia was not a racist place. Those in the know knew of a popular saying around town: "Forsyth was a county that had warned black visitors not to let the Sun go down on your head."

Racial False Flag Alert!!!: In Plain Talk Volume one, I spoke about how some people use racism to their advantage. They exploit stereotypes and past racist history. This is what happened in January of 2009. A couple faced animosity for their support of Barack Obama. They told authorities that they were headed to the January 20th inauguration of Pres. Obama, but had to return because they heard that their house had burned down. They discovered racist graffiti using the phrase: "Your black boy will die!" (referring to Pres. Obama). Considering that this was Forsyth County, Georgia, one of the most conservative counties in the United States, the story didn't seem to be that much of a stretch. Police discovered that it was all a hoax in an effort to defraud the insurance company. When I first learned of the account, I naturally assumed that they were an African-American couple. I was shocked to find out that they were white! To add to the shock, the lady was found with a large amount of cocaine, ready to distribute.

Personal note: I remember doing something similar as a young kid growing up in Brooklyn. Sometimes when an area has an extensive racist past, it becomes very easy for people to exploit situations using race. Every morning before going to school I would stop at Zookey's (a neighborhood store) to play video games. My mother had just brought me an expensive pair of Adidas. They had the thick shoelaces and shell toes, just like I wanted them. For once in my life I had a pair of sneakers that I could be proud of. For some strange reason while playing video games, I sat my sneakers on top of the video-game while playing. I guess you can figure out what happened next. Absentmindedly, in a rush to get to school on time, I left my sneakers in the store. By the time I remembered what I had done, it was too late to turn back, because I would be very late for school. The whole day I began thinking of excuses to tell my mother to try to get out of a beating. Since I knew the history of harassment of black kids by white kids, I decided to use this to my advantage. I told my mother that I was accosted by some white kids who then took my Adidas. From the very beginning, she was skeptical of the story. It wasn't long before the truth came out because I was a horrible liar. I can't even remember if I got a being or not, all I remember is the shame of trying to be a race hustler.

Source: Atlanta Journal Constitution

Cracker Barrel Attack—
Clayton Co. Morrow, Georgia (Sept. 9th 2009)

Cracker Barrel is my favorite place to eat breakfast, but what happened on September 9, 2009, would have been enough to make me lose my appetite. Cracker Barrel, just like Denny's, has had a rocky relationship with diversity. This incident did not help their image.

Troy Dale West swung the door of a Georgia Cracker Barrel open and almost hit the seven-year-old daughter of Tasha Hill. Words were exchanged when Mrs. Hill asked Mr. West to be careful. We don't know exactly what was said, but what happened next is not up for debate. Mr. West began to beat Mrs. Hill viciously in front of her seven-year-old daughter. The whole time, Mrs. Hill was reminding Mr. West that she was an Army reservist. While Mr. West was beating Mrs. Hill, he was yelling profanity and racial slurs like the F-word, N-word, and B-word.

Many people were outraged at the low bail for Mr. West. They felt, due to the nature of his crime, that he should be considered a danger to the public. Originally, he was charged with three misdemeanors and released on $5000 bond. A grand jury later upgraded the charges to felonies. The result was that Mr. West was put back in jail and held without bond. Cracker Barrel also stepped up to the plate by banning Mr. West for life from all of their restaurants. The really disturbing part of this story is the lame excuses given by Mr. West and his supporters as to why he beat Mrs. Hill. He claimed that Mrs. Hill spat on him. The video surveillance tape and eyewitnesses did not back up Mr. West's claims. However, Mr. West's cousin went on CNN's program with Rick Sanchez and said Mr. West was provoked, because he never saw Mr. West hit anyone. He said, if a woman puts herself in a man's shoes, then she may deserve to be hit. Other people in Mr. West's neighborhood also expressed disbelief in his actions. One lady from his neighborhood stressed that Mr. West had a good Christian upbringing. People in the United States, both white and black, and in between, need to stop making excuses for racism. It only makes you look foolish. **(See the letter J. in my ABCs of Racial Rapport)**

Interracial Couple Denied Marriage License
(October 2009)

Sometimes people forget that racism used to be front and center in America. With numerous laws on the books, certain attitudes and actions have gone underground. Well, these attitudes and actions from the Jim Crow era reared its ugly head for all the world to see, when a Louisiana justice of the peace refused to grant an interracial couple a marriage license. His main concern was the offspring of the marriage. In his infinite wisdom, he claimed that interracial marriages do not last long. (It's hard for me to believe that this judge steps within 4 feet of an interracial marriage, in order to investigate the situation.)

Keith Bardwell, the judge who doesn't like race mixing, defensively said: "I am not a racist." "I have piles and piles of black friends." And if you thought that wasn't proof enough, he took it a step further: "I even let them use my bathroom." I don't know about you, but since he lets black people use his bathroom, I know he's not a racist! (Yes, sarcasm is applied.)

You can imagine the embarrassment that Mr. Bardwell brought to the state of Louisiana. Louisiana governor, Bobby Jindal, along with numerous others, called for Bardwell's resignation. Finally, on November 3, 2009, everyone got their wish. I am trying to figure out what's more amazing and unbelievable, the fact that Mr. Bardwell discriminated against this couple and thought it was legal and could get away with it, or that he has turned down four other interracial couples, and no one had turned him in previously. I am sure that Bardwell's community supported his actions in the past, but in today's age, it is certainly not socially acceptable to discriminate. The major positive out of this negative situation, was exposing the racist actions of Mr. Keith Bardwell.

(This section focuses on People)

Arsenio Hall—What Happened?

Way before the Dave Chapelle situation, another puzzling scenario went down with a prominent black TV star. Arsenio Hall had paid his dues on the comedy circuit and earned a spot among the late-night talk show elite. With Jay Leno and David Letterman firmly established in the American psyche, Arsenio boldly went where no other talk show had ever gone. From 1989 to 1994, Arsenio set many trends and introduced the world to new and exciting artists that would never have made it on Johnny Carson's, Jay Leno's, or David Letterman's show. Arsenio became known as the hippest, coolest, and most innovative personality on late-night TV. He started a pop culture phenomenon that consisted of his audience pumping their fists and barking like dogs instead of applauding. Since Arsenio was from Cleveland, it is clear that he got this idea from the infamous dog pound fans of the Cleveland Browns.

Many people affectionately call former Pres. Bill Clinton, the first black president. It was really Arsenio's show, that featured Bill Clinton playing the saxophone, that really started Bill Clinton's persona as a super cool guy. Arsenio was also known for featuring the hottest R&B/hip-hop artists of the day. It was no coincidence that during Arsenio's run as a late-night talk-show host, rap started to really go mainstream. Some revisionists have tried to downplay the significance of Arsenio's accomplishments. I will say that Arsenio's show started to lose some of its luster at the and in 1994, but it was still relevant, especially with the Rodney King riots engulfing the country. I am sure that Arsenio's show would have challenged conventional thinking concerning matters of race. But something happened on Arsenio show that seemed to be an immediate deathblow.

There are many theories as to why Arsenio's show was canceled. Some say Arsenio wanted too much money when he tried to renegotiate a new contract. Some say that Paramount canceled the show due to low ratings. (This doesn't sound right, because Arsenio's show was canceled a few months before his contract actually expired.) The most popular theory, which is what I believe happened, was the appearance of Louis Farrakhan. (Nation of Islam leader) Farrakhan was widely criticized as being an anti-Semite, whose fiery rhetoric made many whites uncomfortable. Since many Jewish people were at the top levels of Paramount Studios, many saw Farrakhan's appearance as a slap in the face to management and the Jewish community. The long-running stereotype has been that if you cross the Jewish community in Hollywood, you can kiss your career goodbye. (Brought out in Plain Talk Volume One) Some say that this is what happened to Mel Gibson after his racist rant against Jews. It would be ridiculous to think that Arsenio did not calculate the risk of having Farrakhan on his show. Like I said, Arsenio was nearing the end of his contract, and may have been thinking about walking away at the end of his contract. Maybe he just wanted to go out with a bang.

By giving Farrakhan a spotlight, Arsenio turned off many affiliates, advertisers, and viewers. I am sure that Arsenio was warned by many people, not to have Farrakhan on his show. As a black man, Arsenio may have resisted anyone telling him what he could and could not do on his own show. Even during Farrakhan's appearance, Arsenio made reference to the immense pressure to not have Farrakhan on his show. I am pretty sure that Arsenio thought long and hard before having Farrakhan on his show. In fact, this show was built up for weeks. To Arsenio's credit, he asked some hard-hitting questions right at the beginning. He asked Farrakhan if he had anything to do with Malcolm X's death. Despite Arsenio's hard-hitting questions, the crowd was very pro-Farrakhan. To Arsenio's credit again, he was very upfront about the backlash and wanted Farrakhan to answer his critics, who accused him of being the new "Black Hitler." Arsenio's interview skills were at its best. As a neutral host, all you can do is ask the questions that people want to know. You can't control the responses and you shouldn't even try to.

Farrakhan directly addressed Arsenio being threatened with the removal of his show. Farrakhan was prophetic in that sense, because in two weeks, Arsenio's show was over. When Farrakhan brought out how many Jews were influential in the slave trade, I am sure this rubbed many Jews the wrong way. I have found that many shows choose to shy away from hard-hitting thought-provoking content. Arsenio's show dedicated the entire hour to an immersion into many intelligent and sensitive issues of the day. After looking at the interview in its entirety, I have a new theory as to why the Arsenio Hall show was canceled. I firmly believe that the Arsenio Hall show was way before it's time. If this show had aired today, nobody would have a huge backlash against it. Instead, people would be hailing this show as a landmark in the discussion of society's ills. Farrakhan was not extremely controversial in his appearance on Arsenio's show, and Arsenio did not kiss up to Farrakhan. Jews should have applauded Arsenio for asking Farrakhan tough questions that I have never heard anyone ask of Farrakhan. The bulk of Arsenio's questions put Farrakhan on record as to many of the issues that Jews wanted to know.

In closing, you would think that the appearance of Farrakhan on anyone's show would be a death knell for them, but such has not been the case. Mike Wallace has given Farrakhan coverage for over 50 years. Barbara Walters and many prominent news shows have featured Farrakhan as well. Their questions follow the same line of reasoning as Arsenio's. What was the difference? The most glaring difference is, that Arsenio's show was not seen as a serious news show, but rather entertainment.

Was Paramount rendering a verdict or ultimatum that said: You are safe as long as you stick to entertainment and non-combative issues, but when you step out of that sphere, all bets are off. What does this say about the control of a few over the masses? Who decides what topics can be covered and catered to the mainstream masses? If Arsenio's show was on BET, would he have suffered such retribution? Since Arsenio's audience reached a wide variety of homes, was that the real danger of his interview with Farrakhan? In other words, if you want the privilege of having a diverse and widespread audience, you better shy away from covering certain issues. If you don't play by those unwritten rules, then you could find yourself on the outside looking in!

James Byrd Jr. (June 7th 1998)

When people think of brutal lynchings, they usually think about the late 1800s and early 1900s. They may have also remembered the infamous lynching postcards made famous because of the sheer surrealism of the images. The casualness of the white onlookers contrasted sharply with the prone mutilated black bodies in the background. Billie Holiday sang many great songs, but her best-selling and most powerful song was "Strange Fruit." This song powerfully captured the horrors of lynchings. Even after anti-lynching laws curtailed these heinous acts, the 1960s saw an uptick in lynchings in the South as a backlash to civil rights activity. But when you think of brutal lynchings, do the 1990's come to mind? Not likely, but that all changed when the world received a wake-up call when James Byrd Junior was brutally drug behind a truck for three miles in Jasper, Texas. This insane act of hate and violence occurred on June 7, 1998.

When details of the crime surfaced, many had to go back to the civil rights movement of the 1960s to relate to the brutality of such a crime. Three white men targeted Mr. Byrd based solely on the color of his skin. Two of the white man were known white supremacists. Mr. Byrd's right arm and head became detached from his body when he hit a concrete conduit. Mr. Byrd's mutilated body was dumped in front of a black cemetery for shock value. After the brutal act, the three white man went to a barbecue. Of the three men, one was 84 while the other two were 31 and 23. The older man received life in prison, while the other two received the death penalty. George W. Bush did not help his status in the black community when he skipped out on Mr. Byrd's funeral. Nor did he endear himself to the black community by opposing hate crime legislation.

Side story: Why do people try to be funny when it comes to racism? It's obvious that those type of jokes are so bad that most people see it as overt racism. Case in point: Doug "The Greaseman" Tracht. Granted, Mr. Tracht is not a household name, however his actions seemed more malicious than that of Michael Richards and The Dog Duane Chapman. As a DJ for WWDC in Washington DC, he made a boneheaded racist comment on Martin Luther King Day. He said: "Why don't we plug four more and get the whole week off." An obvious reference to killing four more influential black leaders to get more days off. He then tried to diffuse the situation by saying: "Come on, now, you know I don't mean nothing." (Reminds me of Mike Greenberg's so-called slip of the tongue when he referred to MLK as Martin Luther Coon King Jr. on January 18, 2010)

That MLK incident did not get The Greaseman fired. However, in February of 1999, (less than a year after Byrd's brutal death) The Greaseman played a clip of a song by Lauryn Hill called *Doo-Wop (That Thing)*. Then he said: "and they wonder why we drag them behind trucks." It was clear that The Greaseman wanted to belittle Lauryn Hill's talent, because she was up for several Grammy awards at the time. This was his second major slipup belittling the life of black people. The first time he was suspended for a week and WWDC gave scholarships to Howard University to alleviate the public outcry. This time, the public demanded his immediate dismissal. You can pretty much guess what came next from The Greaseman. Just like Imus, Michael Richards, The Dog Duane Chapman, and others in similar situations, The Greaseman went on an apology tour. With the loss of his lucrative salary and way of life, he finally realized the error of his ways. He became a pariah in the radio industry. He finally got a job at WFYV-FM in Jacksonville, Florida. (Way to go Jacksonville!!!)

Dave Chappelle—What Happened?

Sometimes people can be so funny, that you have a tendency to excuse behaviors that you would normally say are stereotypical. Eddie Murphy, Richard Pryor, Chris Rock, and so many great African-American comedians have made fun of, and in some cases, reinforced stereotypes of African-Americans. Comedic genius Paul Mooney, would probably be considered the best at taking racial stereotypes and forcing people to nervously laugh at them. Dave Chapelle, an understudy of Paul Mooney, was in the process of making racial satire as American as apple pie.

The Dave Chapelle Show was one of the most popular shows on Comedy Central, and all of cable television during its short three-year run. (2003-2005) The way that Dave Chapelle handled the sticky issue of race was comedic, yet thought-provoking. It was so over-the-top that it challenged people to think: Do other races view me in that way? It also caused many people to think: Do I view other races that badly? One of Dave's sketches that will live forever in people's minds is Clayton Bigsby. Clayton is a blind black KKK member, who doesn't know that he's black. Just seeing a blind black man spewing racist rhetoric against minorities would normally be very distasteful, but the main goal of this sketch was to show everyone how stupid racism is. Everyone seemed to get it. Biting racial satire became a staple on Dave's show until the abrupt end of his show during season three. So the million-dollar question is: What happened?

Dave just signed a $55 million deal with Viacom, which included a piece of DVD sales. (Dave's Chapelle Show DVD became the best-selling TV DVD of all time, beating out The Simpsons.) To everyone, it seemed as if Dave went crazy. Who gives up $55 million! Early reports made it seem as if Dave was on drugs and went to South Africa to get himself clean. As time went on, Dave fully explained why he gave up $55 million and walked away. Dave was unhappy with the direction of the show and felt pressure from network executives to produce mindless racial comedy. He explained that he felt people were laughing "at him" and not "with him." Dave went on to describe some of his skits as "socially irresponsible." To illustrate, he cited the "Pixie Sketch", where pixies would appear on his shoulder to encourage racial stereotypes. Dave even appeared in blackface for this skit. During the filming of this skit, he saw a white crew-member laughing in a way that made him feel uncomfortable. Dave never intended for the Pixie Sketch to air on TV, but Comedy Central aired this skit, and other unfinished material from Dave.

It made me feel uncomfortable watching Dave's fellow TV cohorts host a show without him. Donnel Rawlings and Charlie Murphy seemed to be saying: Sorry you left Dave, but we still got to get paid. Even fellow comedian D.L. Hugley started bashing Dave. D.L. had a short-lived show on Comedy Central called, Weekends on the DL. When the show first came on, D.L. took every opportunity to take potshots at Dave. It almost seemed like it was in D.L.'s contract to bash Dave and mention his name at least five times per show. Once again, it made me feel uncomfortable watching Dave get bashed for showing artistic integrity. You would have thought that Dave would have been applauded in the black community for wanting to put out a product that would help and not harm the image of black people. Instead, these were some other things on people's minds: "I miss Dave's show. Why did he have to leave so abruptly? Dave messed it up for other black comedians!" This type of thinking is selfish and shortsighted. People should have been asking Dave about the changes he would have made to make his show more "socially acceptable." Thank you Dave, for sacrificing fame and fortune in lieu of not being able to look yourself in the mirror everyday and see a real man.

Megan Williams (August 2007) /Channon Christian and Christopher Newsom (January 2007)

As I was researching information about the Megan Williams story, I came across another similar situation: Channon Christian and her boyfriend Christopher Newsom. The Megan Williams case involved a black victim and white perpetrators, and the other crime involved a white couple as victims and five black perpetrators. Several lessons can be learned by examining both accounts closely.

Megan Williams, a 20-year-old black woman from West Virginia, was tortured and sexually abused by six whites in a secluded trailer. The police were able to rescue her after an anonymous tip. She had visible signs of torture and distress on her body. The perpetrators confessed to the crimes and all of their stories corroborated Megan's story. They were not convicted on the word of the victim, but rather their own confessions and physical evidence. Thankfully so, because after some time, Megan Williams recanted her story. Let's just be blunt! Megan has some mental and emotional issues that existed before all of this happened. The physical evidence and confessions stood on their own. The fact that she went back on her story had no bearing on the guilt or innocence of the criminals. The prosecutors sensed that Megan was not a credible witness, so they built their case on other factors. It's sad that some people out there felt that she made everything up because she took her story back. Even after Megan recanted, the criminals in jail still stood by their confessions.

Now let's switch gears and discuss a crime that is almost the polar opposite (in terms of race) of the Megan Williams crime. In the case of Channon Christian and Christopher Newsom, you had two white victims and five black perpetrators.

Christian and Newsom were an attractive young white couple whose simple carjacking in Knoxville, Tennessee turned into a horrific and sadistic episode of rape and murder. There is some dispute as to the exact events of the crime, but it goes without saying that the people behind this crime cannot be classified as human beings. Their actions were straight out of a horror movie. What's really sad is that some white supremacists and right wing extremists tried to use this case as a rallying cry to bring hate crime charges. The premise was that the liberal media shies away from cases that feature white victims and black perpetrators. They cited a few obscure examples and even used the Duke lacrosse incident as a prime example. What these extremists didn't mention, was the biggest media case of the century, the O.J. Simpson trial. Nor did they mention the endless hours of Kobe Bryant coverage. They also failed to take the media to task for focusing so much attention on Paris Hilton, Britney Spears, Kanye West/Taylor Swift, etc. With these petty and meaningless episodes clogging up the airwaves, no wonder there is not enough time to cover issues like the Megan Williams/Christian and Newsom crimes. You can't claim racial bias in the reporting of these two crimes because both the Megan Williams story and the Christian and Newsom story received very little coverage. In fact, the only reason I found out about the Christian and Newsom story was due to researching the Megan Williams story.

There are so many brutal, demonic, horrific, sadistic, and senseless crimes occurring in the world to the point where it is not even sexy for media outlets to cover these type of crimes. It makes you wonder, who really decides what stories to cover. If you look at the statistics that the FBI keeps on crime, you will discover that black people are more likely to be victims of violent crimes in the US (actually more than twice as likely). Obviously, the bulk of these crimes are black on black. But to be fair, if you wanted to call the Christian and Newsom murders a hate crime, then that would be fine by me. But please don't belittle the victims by trying to co-opt tragedies for your own political gain. (i.e. Willie Horton) Certain crimes are so sick, that they should fall into a special category. As long as that category affords for longer and harsher penalties. One of the main reasons why prosecutors don't like to use hate crime laws, is because they are not harsh enough. They just prefer to charge criminals under laws that are already on the books, that provide for harsher penalties. So if you really want to just use "plain talk", all sick and sadistic crimes should be labeled hate crimes for simplicity's sake. But the bottom line that I take away from these two crimes is: don't use crimes to divide people. Because you only dishonor the victims.

Daniel Cowarrt/Paul Schlesselman (foiled 2008 killing spree)

When Barack Obama became president, many people knew the dangers he would face. Membership in hate groups rose all over the United States. Threats were received to the presidency in record numbers. But one threat to the president stood out for it's sheer brutality.

In 2008, there was an assassination plot against then presidential candidate, Barack Obama, that consisted of an inhumane violent killing spree. Two white supremacists (Cowart and Schlesselman) planned to kill 88 African-Americans, while beheading 14 of the 88. (These specific numbers have some sort of purpose among white supremacists) (88 = HH for Heil Hitler and 14 is a white supremacists' 14 word mantra) Supposedly they were going to kill black children at a predominantly black school in Tennessee. Thankfully, smart people are not behind these type of plots. After all of this mayhem, (they didn't plan on getting caught) they were supposed to kill the president by driving at him as fast as they could while shooting. Of course they got caught, because they committed a simple crime, (shooting out a church window) and bragged to a female friend about it. The friend told the cops, and you can guess what happened next. As ridiculous as their plan may sound, it shows what goes on in some people's minds. Some people tried to downplay the severity of the threat, but what if one individual was hurt as a result of these lunatics. That's why you can see why all threats should be taken very seriously.

Tiger Woods—Did Stereotypes play a huge role in the Coverage of his Scandal?

In my first book Plain Talk Volume One, I put forth a media theory called "piling it on." This is where the media turns a story/scandal/episode involving a celebrity of color into a highly polarizing racial event by "piling on the coverage." In other words, the media is negative, excessive, and highly sensationalized in their coverage. When this happens, races began to take sides. Many white people become extremely negative against a celebrity of color, while many black people start to defend the celebrity of color. Many times it does not even matter whether they agree with what the celebrity did or not. Sometimes these celebrities of color are not very supportive of the black community. Some examples of celebrities who have fit into the category of this "piling in on" theory are: Michael Jackson, OJ Simpson, Serena Williams, Kanye West, and more recently Tiger Woods.

The Tiger Woods scandal was bad enough, but with the Vanity Fair cover of February 2010, the scandal was in danger of entering the racial polarization zone. The Vanity Fair cover featured a shirtless Tiger Woods in a skullcap, pumping weights. For the first time, many got to see the darkness of Tiger Woods' skin. To add further insult to injury, on page 22, Vanity Fair had a menacing picture of a profusely sweating Tiger Woods with the caption:Bogey Man-Tiger Woods sweats it out. For those who don't know, a Bogey Man is a monstrous figure used to frighten children, or a dreaded or terrifying figure in general. Despite what people may feel about Tiger's actions, he has done a tremendous amount of charity work for children. I don't know why Vanity Fair chose to take this critisism to a new low. When looking at the online articles of the Tiger Woods story after the Vanity Fair cover came out, I began to notice many white people calling Tiger Woods ugly. They even went so far as to make fun of his dark skin and dark nipples. This was not a tone in which I was accustomed to hearing, concerning Tiger Woods. It was ironic that the same white people who relished the fact that Tiger Woods did not consider himself black were now recognizing his blackness in a negative way. Tiger Woods was not an individual that was known to rock the boat or stir the pot (in a racial sense). When Fuzzy Zoeller made his infamous "fried chicken and collard greens" comment, and, Golf Channel commentator Kelly Tilghman said that "they should lynch Tiger Woods in the back alley", Tiger Woods deflected all questions on race and said let's move on. What did Tiger get for all his efforts: a current scandal replete with racial stereotypes galore.

Tiger did not help himself. As a young immature athlete, he made several off the cuff comments in 1997 to Buzz Bissinger that were sexist and racist. He made crude jokes about lesbians and the size of black men's genitalia. In Volume 1 of Plain Talk, I spoke about how this is a common stereotype often used by black males as a badge of honor, but the origins are not flattering at all. (linked to animals) The timing of the Vanity Fair cover was very suspect because the interview where Tiger made these unfortunate comments were made several years ago. Even the cover photo that was used was old. The premise of putting the article out so late was, to show that this is how Tiger really is. This gives a glimpse or warning of his womanizing ways. The only problem was Vanity Fair never really explained why they waited so long to run the story. Were they paid off? Who knows! The whole Tiger Woods scandal lost a great deal of steam when a massive earthquake hit Haiti. The worlds' attention shifted to something way more important, and rightly so.

Toby Keith—Oslo Norway (December 11, 2009)

In Plain Talk Volume one, I wrote about Miley Cyrus and Joe Jonas slanting their eyes to look Chinese. I also wrote about how the Spanish National/ Olympic basketball team took a photo doing the same thing. Finally, I commented on how Rosie O'Donnell was also chided for making fun of the way Asians speak. Despite all of this information out there, it seems that Toby Keith. didn't get the memo.

Of all places, Toby Keith chose to be racially insensitive at a Nobel Peace Prize after-party. He joined the stage as Will Smith rapped the classic "Rappers' Delight." When the lyric: "I like to say hello, to the white to the black the red and brown, the purple and *yellow*", came up in the song, Toby's brain must have shut down. Because when Will Smith said "*yellow*", Toby was seen to point to his eye in an effort to draw attention to the slanted eyes of Asians. He may even have physically slanted his eye, but the video is unclear. His actions went unnoticed due to the reverie and merriment of the occasion, but soon the video went viral over the Internet. Just like anyone caught being racially insensitive, Toby, his supporters, and staff went into spin mode.

Here is a quote from a representative of the Asian-American Justice Center:

> **"Toby Keith embarrassed himself and his country, denigrated the Nobel Peace Prize, and offended Asians and Asian-Americans by using a crude and racist hand gesture".**

Here's the spin from Toby's camp:

> **"No one at the concert thought Toby was out of line. Everyone was impressed with his rapping skills and that's it. All of the artists liked each other, hung out, and it was a very friendly, genuine, and supportive atmosphere".**

Well here's my point, why even put your hands anywhere near your eyes when "*yellow*" is being mentioned in the song? Maybe Toby did not feel that this was a racist gesture, but when he found out it offended Asians, he should have immediately apologized. Disappointingly, he did not. Also the spin about "no one at the concert thought Toby was out of line" is suspect. The concert was in Norway, not Hong Kong. If he had done this in San Francisco or Seattle, or anywhere else where there is a heavy Asian presence, someone would have noticed and called him out for his actions.

Jesse James (March—April 2010)

I had no idea who Jesse James was. The only reason I heard about him was due to his cheating on his beautiful wife, actress Sandra Bullock. To make matters worse, he cheated on his wife with a stripper and tattoo model. To make matters even worse than that, the woman he cheated with had racist photos of her in a Nazi hat and swastika armband surface on the Internet. Just when you thought things couldn't get any worse, Jesse James had a photo of himself in the same Nazi hat, making the Hitler salute (Heil Hitler), and putting two fingers over his mouth to mimic Hitler's mustache.

Spin Alert!!!: According to Jesse's lawyer, the Nazi hat was a gift from a Jewish mentor, so that excuses him from being a Neo-Nazi. Also, the photo of James posing as Hitler, was a joke according to his lawyer. Where's the joke in emulating a vile person responsible for the deaths of millions. To me that makes it even worse!! This goes back to my original premise in Plain Talk Volume one: Nobody wants to be called a racist. They will do and say anything to deflect that label. It is the absolute worst label, other than a child molester, that you could call someone. Jesse James has yet to take full responsibility for his hateful actions.

CHAPTER FIVE

Augusta Life

In Plain Talk Volume 1, very little reference was made to Augusta, GA. Since we are "digging a little deeper", it is important to get some insight on the city where I dwell. It may hold the "real" key, as to why the Plain Talk Series was born.

A Break from the Norm. Augusta—Georgia's Second Largest (underachieving) City.

I am a frequent visitor to Savannah, Georgia. I would have to put Savannah in my top five cities to visit. As I write this, I have spent two days in downtown Savannah and on the riverfront. Every time I come to Savannah, I can't help but think: What if? What if Augusta's riverfront was as developed as Savannah's? What if Augusta would fully develop its rich history in the form of a bus or trolley tour? The "what ifs" go on and on. There are no shortage of good progressive ideas in Augusta, Georgia. These are some of the ideas that have been bantered about:

1) **South Augusta's own racetrack—Marion Williams**
2) **Augusta's own waterpark**
3) **Turning the Augusta Canal into a water street, similar to what they have in Venice, Italy.(complete with gondolas or water taxis)**
4) **Downtown baseball stadium on the river—this stadium would be for the Augusta Greenjackets, owned by baseball Hall of Famer Cal Ripken Jr.**

5) **James Brown Museum—some suggest turning his home in Beech Island S.C. into a sort of Graceland. Another good idea that I have heard is to make a Hard Rock Cafe styled museum dedicated to James Brown and his musical legacy.(based on a model in the lobby of the White Building)**
6) **Trolley (Streetcar) line running in downtown Augusta—this trolley would be modeled after the one in Portland Oregon. Tracks would have to be built, which of course makes the cost a major factor. No exhaust and no gas cost, would be a major plus.**
7) **Large outdoor amphitheater in South Augusta—this amphitheater would be a lot larger than the Jesse Norman amphitheater on the Riverwalk in downtown Augusta.**

Amphitheater named after one of the greatest
Opera singers alive, Jessye Norman.

8) **Regency Mall—fill in the blank.**

This is just a sampling of the ideas that have been thrown out there for public consumption. No matter what ideas are thought of, people began to look at the economics and how will this benefit my community. Unfortunately, many people see ***my*** community as **white** and **black** community.

When communities have rivers that run in close proximity to a city, they usually use this prime real estate to the full. I can think of at least four cities that do this:

1) **San Antonio, Texas—this city has one of the most beautiful riverfront centers of activity in the United States**
2) **Fort Lauderdale, Florida—even though they have the ocean, they have utilized the river as well.**
3) **Louisville, Kentucky—one of my most memorable memories of Louisville, along with the Muhammad Ali center, would have to be the beautiful river and the old-fashioned pipe organ playing near a steamboat.**
4) **Savannah, Georgia—just like Fort Lauderdale, even though Savannah has the ocean, they have developed the Savannah Riverfront into an attraction that is a must see when you visit town.**

Street performer in front of a bustling riverfront crowd in Savannah, Ga. If Augusta commercially develops it's riverfront, then street performers may come to perform in Augusta. (This guy was from New Orleans)

The same river that has been built around Savannah, is in Augusta. Augusta could model their Riverwalk after Savannah's. The only thing on the river in Augusta is basically the Riverwalk. Fort Discovery, a hands on science center, is in the process of leaving the Riverwalk area. Augusta needs to build directly onto River. You should be able to eat at several restaurants and look out the window and see the Savannah River. Some have even suggested sectioning off an area and making it an artificial beach. Whatever the case, Augusta needs to fully develop and utilize the Savannah River to the full!

Augusta's riverfront needs more commercial development to take advantage of the natural beauty of the Savannah River.

Augusta has rich history. At one time it used to be the capital of Georgia. Also, there are several historical landmarks spread out all throughout the city. When you go to cities like Savannah, they utilize their rich history by developing several sightseeing tours around the city by bus/trolley. Augusta has the rich history to do the same thing. Augusta's tour could actually be spread out more geographically than Savannah's tour. You have the historical African-American districts in the Laney Walker area. In the same area you also have a Black history Museum. You also have Paine College and Frank Yerby's house all in the same vicinity. Erskine Caldwell's Tobacco Road could also be a feature of the tour. The downtown Broad Street area is actually America's second widest street behind New Orleans' Bourbon Street. Downtown also has the Augusta Museum of History, Morris Museum of Art, Augusta Commons, James Brown statue, slave pole, Augusta Canal, Ezekiel Harris House, Woodrow Wilson's boyhood home, and many other points of interest. There are also historical districts around Augusta State University, which later became used as the Augusta Arsenal.

Up until this point, I have yet to mention Augusta's biggest draw: the Augusta National on Washington Road, home of the PGA Masters golf tournament. Unfortunately, the Augusta National is closed to the general public. One private citizen of Augusta, Grady Abrams, has made a brilliant case to convince the upper brass of the Augusta National to open the Masters course up to the general public for tours. The tours would run during the course's downtime of course. Let's hope someone runs with Grady's idea.

So in summary, Augusta, Georgia, the second-largest metropolitan area in Georgia, is not living up to its potential. There are three strong areas that separate Augusta from all other cities:

1) **Augusta's portion of the Savannah River—(which is directly across from North Augusta, South Carolina) North Augusta is equally capable of developing their side of the river. This is something that Augusta has over Savannah. Savannah does not have any other cities surrounding it that are developed. Augusta not only has North Augusta, but they also have Aiken, South Carolina and Columbia County as well.**

North Augusta should build more than just lavish homes on their side of the river. They could use the commercial development to boost their economy.

2) **Augusta is rich and unique history—Augusta has been pivotal to Georgia's history for some time. The Augusta Canal is a US treasure. It is the only Canal in the United States still used for its original purpose. Downtown and the surrounding areas are ripe with interesting history. Scott Hudson, a private citizen of Augusta, came up with an interesting article examining Augusta's lucrative Black history points of interests. And to top it all off, one of Augusta's native sons is known all over the world. (James Brown—the Godfather of soul, Soul Brother number one, etc.) Something should be done to incorporate all of the historical points of Augusta, maybe in the form of a coordinated sightseeing tour.**

Unfortunately, this is all that many people get to see of the Augusta National. Does it have to be that way? Not according to Grady Abrams.

3) **The Augusta National—home of the Masters golf tournament. People all over the world love to be a part of the atmosphere of the Masters. Grady Abrams' idea of using this viable asset to the benefit of all of Augustans is a very enticing one. I have been told many times that the television coverage does not do justice to the aesthetic beauty of the Augusta National golf course. Maybe one day I will get to find out if that statement is an exaggeration or not.**

In order for Augusta to grow, everyone needs to feel a part of the team. Projects should not be approached from the standpoint of "what would benefit one race or one side of town over another". People should see through the politics to see how something benefits all citizens of Augusta.

If you know the infrastructure of Savannah, you can see that the African-American community lives separately from the Riverfront area. What if projects came up to develop areas outside of the African-American community, say on the river, should the African-American community try to railroad these projects? If that would be the case, then nothing would get done. When one part of Savannah flourishes, jobs are available for all citizens of Savannah, regardless of color. Along the same note, apply that same theory to Augusta. If dollars flow to one area, and it is successful, then all will benefit. The problem is including everyone into the process, or getting private entities to invest their own money instead of asking taxpayers to foot the bill. People will be watching the TEE Center in Augusta to see if it will be a bust or boom. If the TEE Center is a bust, it will discourage businesses from investing in downtown Augusta. If the TEE Center is a huge success or boom, then it will bring more jobs for all citizens of Augusta. So when it comes to business development, we should not see things in black and white, but rather in black and red.

The Augusta Chronicle: The only game in town.

The Augusta Chronicle is the city of Augusta's only daily newspaper. Across the Savannah River you have the Aiken Standard. Once a week you have the Metro Spirit, Metro Courier, and a slew of other specialized periodicals. Once upon a time, you had the Augusta Focus, run by the Walker family. More recently, there was a magazine called U magazine, that catered to the black community. Their last issue came out in January of 2010. So there are other newspapers in town, but the Augusta Chronicle is considered the flagship for daily news in the Augusta area.

With that being said, you would think that the Augusta Chronicle would take the job or should I say responsibility of being the only game in town a little more seriously. Without looking at statistics, it is safe to say that the city of Augusta is inhabited by a majority of African-Americans. However, if you were to read the Augusta Chronicle on a day-to-day basis, you would never know this to be true.

The Augusta Chronicle is run by the Morris family. It has been that way for many years. The paper reflects the right wing conservative views of this owner William "Billy" Morris, just like Fox news reflects the views of its owner, Rupert Murdoch. There is nothing wrong with the paper's editorial staff being conservative, liberal, or in between. The problem lies when the Augusta Chronicle does not allow opposing views to be published as a rebuttal to their conservative views. Unlike Fox news, which has CNN and MSNBC to counter their views on a daily basis, the Augusta Chronicle has no competing daily newspaper. So in effect, many times the Augusta Chronicle has pushed a conservative right wing agenda without rebuttals from the community that it serves.

What examples do I have to back up my claims? The most glaring deficiency of the Augusta Chronicle has to do with a lack of writers who are people of color. The racial makeup of the staff does not reflect the community in which it serves. I am not saying that William Morris is racist, but his paper is not as good as it can be, due to lack of imagination or diversity. (Take your pick.) Another deficiency deals with the editor of the editorial section, Mike Ryan. I don't know Mr. Ryan personally, but those that do have said that he is a nice man. The question that I have is: How unbiased can you claim to be as an editorial staff, when your head guy speaks at Tea Party rallies? If you are going to be unabashedly slanted in your views, at least field criticism from opposing views. Is it too much to ask the editorial staff of the Augusta Chronicle to show some magnanimity! It seems as if the editorial staff takes their talking points directly from Fox news. Show some originality! How many times can you bash Pres. Obama? How many times can you tell us the government is spending too much money? (Somehow they always find a way to tie this trait to Democrats) No wonder the Augusta Chronicle is on its last financial legs; it sounds like a broken record.

Another example that I would like to highlight is the press release of the AABA. (All American Basketball Alliance) It seemed weird that the Chronicle and Billy Byler were the first to break this story nationally. To add insult to injury, they broke this story on Martin Luther King Day. Did other news outlets have this press release? If you know anything about press releases, you know that press releases are sent out in mass. Were other outlets waiting to break the story of a segregated basketball league at a more appropriate time? Probably so! Way to go Augusta Chronicle for putting Augusta on the national sports map way before April!

When the Chronicle ran the story of the all white basketball league, they ran a short piece condemning the league as well. The Chronicle was willing to give Don "Moose" Lewis, the creator of the AABA a national spotlight, and then played the good guy by bashing this league at the same time. When I saw the rebuttal by Scott Micheaux of the Augusta Chronicle, it seemed to be lacking in substance. I set forth to write a strong detailed repudiation of the AABA, that was very specific to the Augusta area. I sent this open letter to the Augusta Chronicle, but they refused to print it. The stance that they took was: it's time to move on. I wonder if they will give Don "Moose" Lewis any publicity when he comes back trying to push his league on the Augusta area. If they do, then it shows that the Augusta Chronicle wants to control the flow of information. I guess those perks come with the territory when you are the only game in town.

On a side note, the Augusta Chronicle could do more to support local artists. They should have a section that people could look to where they feature only local writers, musicians, artists, etc. Instead, the Chronicle features generic AP stories about national books and artists, that you can read any time online. Those writers and artists who are featured could care less about Augusta. When you buy their products, your money does not go back into the local economy. It would make more sense and cents to feature local artists on a more regular basis instead of the generic AP articles. Every Sunday instead of featuring a local book review, we get a generic book review from the AP that features writers that we will never see in our lives. If local artists were featured on a more regular basis, people can learn more about them, and it is a good chance that you may even run into them when you're around town. Since people can interact with local artists, their stories are way more compelling than generic AP stories. Readership would probably go up, because local artists and their families would buy more newspapers. Also, local artists will spend more money towards the local economy. With increased publicity comes increased sales. With increased sales comes a more vibrant local economy. Many times local artists feature their products in local Mom and Pop stores. The downtown scene in Augusta is notorious for featuring local artists. Everybody wins with this scenario, the Augusta Chronicle, local artists, readers of the Augusta Chronicle, and local businesses. Unfortunately, I pitched this idea to the Augusta Chronicle but they gave me the cold shoulder. I guess you can do that when you are the only game in town. Well I guess I refuse to play this game so I'm going to take my wallet and go home.

Why go to McDonald's or Burger King, when you can go to Dixie Burger!!! (only in the Valley)

Klan Rally in Gloverville, South Carolina (April 3rd 2010)

When you think of Klan rallies, most people think about the 3R's: Robes, Rebel flags, and Racist Rhetoric. (Okay, maybe four R's) Also if you are a student of history, you have visions of the 50s and 60s where the Klan burned crosses and issued fiery mantras. Of course, we are living in different times where people are not welcomed to be so overt when it comes to racism. This still do not stop me from thinking that I would see the 3R's as I went back to where I spent four years of my childhood, Gloverville, South Carolina.

Gloverville has always been an enigma to me. I could sense that many of the folks in the "Valley" area, had been brain washed. Most of the brain washed were poor and frustrated. Instead of focusing or channeling their energies for the betterment of their plight, they chose to worry about other races. I still have fond memories of Gloverville South Carolina, as I attended LBC middle school and my first two years of high school at Midland Valley. (The year after I left Midland Valley to go to Butler HS in Augusta, Georgia, they had major race problems at Midland Valley) One incident in the Valley area stands out in my mind and will stay with me for as long as I live. As a teenager, I was walking near a Gurley's supermarket in the Valley and saw a white man in his 20s walking with his little son. I saw the man whisper something to his son, almost as if he were coaching the little boy. As I walked by them within earshot, I heard the little boy point at me and say: **Look Daddy, a Nigger!** I just shook my head and kept walking. Like I said, these people have been brain washed. Another incident stood out that took place in middle school. (LBC) In art class, we were drawing pictures that represented our life. Well this one kid proceeded to draw a sick racist picture that showed the KKK lynching black people. This was no stick figure drawing. It had color and racist dialogue as well. The detail was so exact, that you couldn't help but think that this kid had been to a lynching himself. So I cited these two examples to explain why I expected the worst when I went to the Klan rally in Gloverville, South Carolina.

At the Klan rally, there were more people observing from a distance, than they were people at the actual rally. They did not seem too eager to associate themselves with the Klan. As you got closer, you could see the leader of the local Klan movement, Tim Bradly, holding court. All of the major local media outlets were in attendance: Channel 12s Blayne Alexander, Ken J. Makin from the Metro Courier, the Augusta Chronicle, News 26's Mrs. O'Donnell (NBC), and many others. I only saw one rebel flag and no robes. (It was later explained that the robes would be put on at a private initiation at an undisclosed farm.) (AKA Cross Burning) It was good to see other white people verbally challenging the rhetoric of the Klan. There were a few verbal spats, but nothing violent or out of control. Everything seemed to be very civil. (Heavy police presence, including several black police, probably had something to do with that.)

The one thing that I will really take away from this rally, is the attempt to dress up the Klan to resemble the tenants of the Tea Party movement. Gone was the emphasis on Black people and Jews. The main focal point seemed to be Mexicans and illegal immigration. The immigration debate may get more people riled up than the health-care reform debate. (If you can believe that!) The new Klan wants to keep the robes and cross burnings regulated to private areas. They know that style of intimidation is only fodder for the media to bash them. They are now careful to not use racial slurs in public, for they know they will drive white people away in droves. The new Klan is more low key and media savvy than the old Klan. I even heard Tim Bradly, leader of the local Klan movement, say that he wanted to work with the NAACP. A photo was even orchestrated that showed Mr. Bradly shaking hands with a young black man from Augusta. As the young black man saw that someone took a photo of him shaking hands with a Grand Wizard of the KKK, he began to see the gravity of the situation. He expressed fear of retribution in his neighborhood, if word got out of what he did. I was hoping that they would not publish the photo, but I saw that it was featured in the Aiken Standard.

I'll just leave you with this last question for you to think about: Is the new Klan more dangerous than the old Klan? (Not in a violent way, but in a battle for people's minds kind of way) Only time will tell!

1970 race riot of Augusta—Let's not forget the past!

When I wrote Plain Talk Volume one, I must admit that I wrote it from a national perspective. I did not have a regional or local mindset. But when I began to be asked by many in the community, why I wrote this book, the tone began to feel like that of people saying: "don't stir the pot" or "you are causing divisions among the races." Many people have an out of sight, out of mind mentality. Many people strongly believe in the phrase: see no evil, hear no evil, speak no evil, when it comes to talking about racism and stereotypes. That still leaves the "think no evil" part out of the equation. For years, some people had mistakenly thought that race relations have gotten better because of the passage of time. They don't realize, that in order for some things to change, some ugly incidents have had to errupt. Usually, these incidents occur, because people neglect festering issues regarding common decency and fair play. All human beings want equal treatment and respect. When those needs are not being met, then the voices start to protest, events began to transpire, and if nothing is done about the matter, then radical elements take over. At that point, all voices of reason have been drowned out, and lack of hope and despair began to take over. Don't worry, I have a very vivid real-life example to prove everything I just said. The incident: the race riot of May 11, 1970. The place: not Newark, New Jersey, Detroit, Michigan, or Watts, California. We are talking about good old Augusta, Georgia.

From studying history, I remember the turmoil and hopelessness of the inner city after the murder of Martin Luther King Jr. Riots broke out all over the US. Even after unrest from the MLK incident died down, there was still unrest in many cities. 1970 proved to be another bloody year. Before these events in 1970, you had a precursor in the Orangeburg, South Carolina massacre. I went to South Carolina State University in Orangeburg for two years, so this event was a stark reminder of the brutal conditions of the past. Even though the Orangeburg massacre was the first extremely violent event on a college campus of this nature, it received very little media attention. Many give the reason for the discrepancy in media attention due to the fact that you had young African-Americans protesting the local segregation of a bowling alley. In any case, the students protesting started a bonfire to keep warm. The police arrived to put the fire out. One of the officers became injured by something thrown. In retaliation, the police began to fire on the crowd. The protesters did not have guns as the police suggested, the only thing thrown at the cops were objects and insults. I'm not condoning the throwing of anything at law enforcement, but the return of deadly force in this situation was obviously excessive. The result: three young men dead—Samuel Hammond, Delano Middleton, and

Henry Smith. Also, the unborn child of Louise Kelly Cawley died as a result of the beatings she received by police, while she was trying to help the injured get to the hospital. In all, 31 people were injured in what then governor of South Carolina, Robert E. McNair called: "one of the saddest days in the history of South Carolina." Unfortunately, Gov. McNair blamed the deaths on outside Black Power agitators, even though there were no indications that this was the case. (Later, Gov. Lester Maddox of Georgia, made similar claims of communist outside agitators being the cause of the riot in Augusta, Georgia of 1970.) At the trial, all nine police officers were acquitted of any wrongdoing. The only person convicted in connection with this crime was Cleveland Sellers, an activist with the student nonviolent coordinating committee (SNCC). 25 years later, Mr. Sellers was pardoned and earned a Master's in education degree from Harvard, a doctorate in history from UNC Greensboro, and is now president of Voorhees College in Denmark, South Carolina.

That whole episode gives you a backdrop of some of the frustrations of the black community and the subsequent mis-application of the causes of the problems by the white government. Now let's spring forward to May 4, 1970, on the campus of Kent State in Ohio, where you have four students dead and nine wounded. Once again, the students were unarmed. Also, there were suspicious allegations of a mysterious sniper in the crowd. This was used as an excuse by the Ohio National Guard for firing on a crowd of unarmed students. This is very suspicious, because the people that died were at an average distance of 345 feet away from the national guards. We are talking about shooting high powered rifles into a crowd of kids.

Before we get into the Augusta riot, let's jump ahead three days to the Jackson State riots in Jackson, Mississippi. On May 14-15th, in the year of 1970, a group of student protesters were fired on by the police. A barrage of 140 shots in 30 seconds were directed toward the young students. Two young men, Philip Lafayette Gibbs (age 21), and James Earl Green (age 17) were killed. 12 people were injured. Can you guess why the police said they fired on the crowd? That's right, the ubiquitous, mysterious, ever elusive sniper was the reason once again. However, no sniper or evidence of gun play by any student protester was ever found.

Right about now, some may feel that I'm talking about some third world country or maybe even Communist China. No, this all happened right here in the United States of America. That's probably why some countries cast a suspicious eye when Americans look down on their country for civil or human rights violations. Now as I talk about the Augusta incident in 1970, see if you notice any similarities from the preceding events.

Grady Abrams' artistic rendition of the
Committee of Ten holding a rally.

To get the inside scoop of the situation, I interviewed Grady Abrams in his art gallery in the back of his home. I asked Mr. Abrams if there were any foreboding events that occurred before the riot. I learned of his arrest by two plainclothes detectives, that was later thrown out of court. It is interesting to note that in Plain Talk Vol. One, I wrote about the phrase "contempt of cop", and how this probably led to the arrest of Henry Louis Gates Junior. What Grady Abrams described sounded like arrest for "contempt of cop." As a result of this incident, Mr. Abrams and his friends spoke with the Sheriff about unacceptable treatment by law enforcement in the black community and became known as "the Committee of 10." This group of black men became known around the black community for their activism. Before the riot, there was a murder in February of 1970, of a cop in Allen Homes, in Augusta, Georgia. Mr. Abrams encountered some Black Panther members trying to get members of the community to riot in the presence of the police. Mr. Abrams realized that this was a lose-lose situation. A heated discussion ensued between Abrams and the leader of the Black Panthers. From that point on, there were tensions between the Committee of 10 and the Black Panthers.

So one day, Mr. Abrams gets a call from May's Funeral Home to come and view a body. It was the body of 16-year-old mentally disabled Charles Oatman. The authorities claimed that he fell off his bunk bed and was involved in some roughhousing during a card game with other inmates. (In our day and age, one automatically questions, why a 16-year-old was in an environment with hardened adult criminals.) So when Willie Mays pulled back the sheet to expose the body of Charles Oatman, what Mr. Abrams saw next appalled him. Charles Oatman's body was covered in cigarette burns, fork marks were all over his body, three gashes about a foot long were in his back, and his skull was busted open. How did the guards leave prisoners unattended for so long, that injuries of this nature occurred? This was an immediate and logical question that came to many people's minds.

So after seeing all of this, Grady Abrams went on his local radio show at James Brown's former station, WRDW, to tell his audience what he had just seen. He told the public to meet him at the jail, because he wanted answers from the sheriff as to what had happened to Charles Oatman. Mr. Abrams and Charles Harris, another local black politician, spoke to officials and received the same story about the card game. So efforts were made to return the next day on Monday, May 11 to meet with city council chairman, Matthew Mulherin, to discuss moving other youths away from adults in the jailhouse. As they were talking, a crowd started to form outside of the courthouse on Greene Street. Mr. Abrams went down to address a restless crowd, that was ready for action. Efforts were made to move the crowd to 9th and Gwinnett St. for a rally. As the crowd started to disperse, one person took it upon themselves to throw a rock at a passing city bus. Unfortunately, more people joined in and now you have a full scale riot on your hands. Rocks were being throw at white people and then people turned their attention to businesses. Fires were burning all over town. Mr. Abrams was quick to point out that he had sensed from his previous encounters with the Black Panthers in Allen Homes, that there was an element looking for a reason to riot. On May 11, they finally got their opening. One of the more symbolic moments of the riot, was when someone climbed the pole at the county municipal building and tore down the Georgia state flag (which at the time still contained the Confederate flag). After snatching the flag down, someone then proceeded to burn the flag. Eventually, the National Guard had to be brought in. Gov. Lester Maddox's whole spin on the cause of the riots was a so-called 40 year old conspiracy by outside agitators. (Communists) This was a sentiment commonly expressed by many white conservatives at the time. No doubt influenced by Sen. McCarthy and the Red Scare of the 1950s. While there may have been a very small communist influence among some of the upper management of the civil rights movement, the people doing the rioting could care less about political affiliations. Most in the black community agreed that tensions boiled over because they were tired of being told that there were no race relations problems in Augusta, Georgia.

Many in the black community, including Grady Abrams, tried to express this sentiment way before the race riot of 1970. Unfortunately, the only time white politicians, law enforcement, and businessmen were willing to talk, was after six black men were shot in the back, 80 injuries, 200 arrests, and 50 destroyed businesses. (Once again, the cops claimed a mysterious sniper was shooting at them.) Finally, all races in Augusta had to agree that there were race related problems. As a result, the Human Relations Commission was formed and future State Sen. Charles Walker became the first director. Race problems continued to linger in Augusta, because in 1972, a federal judge forced the Richmond County Board of Education to desegregate by busing.

We are quickly approaching the 40th year anniversary of the Augusta race riot of 1970. (May 11, 2010) How will history remember this incident? Will people remember the attitudes that existed before the riot occurred? There was a false utopian or Pollyanna type attitude of: "nothing is wrong." In the community there is still a segment that wants to put on airs of perfect racial tolerance. I realize that there are more races on this planet than black and white. In actuality, you have to be more tolerant now than you did in the 70s. Why? Because you have so many more cultures in Augusta now. There are also many bi-racial relationships and children in Augusta. It's not just black and white anymore. There are so many different facets of the Augusta community to embrace. So this blast from the past may be painful for many to remember, but please just take this as a kindly reminder. I am not trying to be a rabble-rouser or agitator; I just believe in the old adage that: Those who don't remember the past, are condemned to repeat it.

Why go Backward? (Stop living in the Past!) An open letter to Don "Moose" Lewis, the Augusta community, and the world at large.

Regardless of what you think about Martin Luther King Day, many recognize that day as a time to reflect on how far the United States has come concerning race relations. So when a news story came out of the Augusta Chronicle on Martin Luther King day of 2010, most people thought it was a sick joke. Don "Moose" Lewis, the commissioner of an all-white basketball league, released a press release to the Augusta Chronicle, that expressed interest in Augusta, Georgia as one of the cities for this all-white league.

According to the press release of the AABA (All-American Basketball Alliance), the only players who qualify are "natural born US citizens with both parents of the Caucasian race". When asked why the restriction on color, Lewis said that the NBA is shutting out many white players. Lewis wants the AABA to focus on basketball fundamentals instead of the typical "streetball" played by "people of color." Lewis cited recent events involving the gun charges of Gilbert Arenas and past events in the NBA involving black players as a reason for an all-white league. Lewis claims that it will be automatically safer for patrons if all of the players are white. He goes on to state that fans would not have to worry about players flipping them off, attacking them, or grabbing their crotch. (Don't go to a baseball or hockey game) it's obvious that Lewis is referring to the incident at the Palace in Auburn Hills, Michigan, where Ron Artest, Jermaine O'Neil, and Stephen Jackson of the Indiana Pacers got into physical altercations with white Detroit Pistons fans in the stands. What Lewis fails to mention is that it was the drunken and obnoxious behavior of the fans that provoked the incident. (Someone threw a cup of beer at Ron Artest.) Clearly, those NBA players crossed the line, but those fans also went way beyond being spectators.

Let's look at Lewis' other line of reasoning for wanting an all-white league, the issue of streetball versus fundamentals. While it is true that the NBA has its share of showmen, those who are the best players know when to hotdog and went to stick to the fundamentals. Players like Magic Johnson, Isiah Thomas, and Michael Jordan come to mind. They were very flashy at times, but very effective. They worked on basketball fundamentals first, then they developed and honed their skills in order to even have the option of performing more complex maneuvers. When the game was on the line, they were all business. My favorite player, Dominique Wilkins, was known as one of the most flamboyant players in the NBA. However, his greatest moment, was a duel with the fundamentally sound, Larry Bird. In game seven of the 1988 NBA Eastern Conference Semi-Finals, these two small forwards went back and forth and played a game of basketball at such a high level, that it moved the legendary and fundamentally sound coach, Red Auerbach to declare: "Greatest quarter I ever saw in 42 years in the NBA." Then you have non-flashy black players like: Kareem Abdul Jabbar, Craig Hodges, Tim Duncan, Oscar Robertson, and even Wilt Chamberlain. All of these players were very fundamentally sound in their positions. On the other hand, you have flashy white players like: Pistol Pete Maravich, Steve Nash, Jason Williams (white chocolate), Da Professor (streetball And One legend), Rex Chapman, and Brent Barry(the only white winner of a NBA slam dunk contest-1996).

I mention all of these players to show that you cannot categorize basketball fundamentals according to race. According to Lewis, he subscribes to the Jimmy "the Greek" Synder theory of blacks being "natural athletes." He says people of color can "make up for their shortfall in fundamentals, with their natural athleticism." (He has obviously never heard of Harold Miner.) Let's be perfectly clear. You have to be fundamentally sound to make it to the professional level of any sport. Coaches want people who are going to help them win. It's not like in college, where you are limited to selecting from your student body. Professional leagues attract the best players. If all of those players happen to be white, then so be it. If they happen to be all black, same rule applies. If there is a mixture races, then so be it. As long as you put together the best team, that's all that counts.

With Augusta's murky and tempestuous past concerning race relations, one begs to wonder: Why select Augusta? Ray Charles refused to perform at the Bell Auditorium in Augusta, Georgia because of segregation. When they agreed to desegregate, he came back and fulfilled his obligation. Desegregation of education has also been very messy here in Augusta. Even in 1899 (Cumming versus Richmond County Board of Education), this issue garnered national attention, going all the way to the Supreme Court. This case shot down an attempt to close white high schools until they reopened black ones. This was three years after Plessy versus Ferguson, which gave us the "separate but equal" doctrine, thus clearing the way for state imposed segregation. With Brown versus Board of Education of Topeka in 1954 making segregated schools illegal under the "equal protection" clause of the law, how would Augusta respond to this landmark case? Not very well!

The Richmond County school system had to be sued by a group of private citizens to force them to desegregate the schools. That was in 1964, 10 years after Brown versus Board of Education. It wasn't until the 1970s, that Augusta's Board of Education finally came up with a plan for desegregation. As of this writing, Augusta is still under a federal court order for the desegregation of its schools.

We have not even mentioned one of Augusta's ugliest racial incidents, the riot of May 1970. We are approaching the 40th year anniversary of the riot. On May 11, 2010, Augusta will mark the anniversary, not with joy and celebration, but with somber reflection and forethought. With all of these issues of the past, not to mention the current uncertainty of the racial make up of the County Commission, do you think Augusta is ready for an all-white basketball league? If you think so, please go back and read this article over from the beginning. In fact, keep reading it until you join the rest of us in the present, and stop living in the past!

The Joke's on Me!!
(and everyone else who paid attention to Don Moose Lewis)

When I first wrote my open letter to Don Moose Lewis, the Augusta community, and the world at large, I began to have any eerie feeling that I was part of a con game. The whole scheme just seemed so convenient. A promoter from Atlanta comes out of nowhere and proposes an all-white basketball league on Martin Luther King Day. A newspaper from Augusta known for its divisiveness in the community decides to run with this story. Both parties benefited by receiving national attention. Both parties are quoted in newspapers all over the world. I personally reached out to Don Moose Lewis to find out if this was some publicity stunt or if he was really serious about bringing such a league to Augusta. He sent me a Facebook message saying that as soon as all the hoopla died down he would contact me. Well, he never did. After many attempts to contact Mr. Lewis, I finally gave up. I began to scour the Internet in hopes of finding an interview that Mr. Lewis gave that confirmed my fears. Well, I finally found that interview. The following is a direct quote from an interview that Mr. Lewis gave to Creative Loafing, a website out of Atlanta:

(Courtesy of Creative Loafing)

Is the league gonna happen, or is it just a publicity stunt? Well, yes and yes. It's absolutely going to happen, he insists. He says the response has been overwhelmingly positive and he thinks he can get 2,000 to 3,000 spectators at games. But he also copped to the gimmickiness of the league's whites-only requirement. He wouldn't be getting any attention from the media, he says, if his announcement about a new league didn't say the league was whites-only. "I had a conventional league for a year-and-a-half. I lost a ton of money," he says. "The press release is basically to garner press. It worked. I've slashed my advertising budget because I don't need it anymore," he says, noting a crew from "The Daily Show with Jon Stewart" (which he calls "The Jon Daily Show") will be interviewing him this week. In other words, Lewis believes he's using the media's shock, horror and condescension to his advantage.

So there you have it, straight from the Moose's mouth! Someone needs to ask the Augusta Chronicle some serious questions. The first being, why in the world did you give this guy a major spotlight? Before I approached Ben Hasan to print my open letter about the all-white basketball league, I approached the Augusta Chronicle. I let everybody who was somebody at the Augusta Chronicle know about this open letter. I even had a prominent member of the community who has her own radio talk show to petition the Augusta Chronicle for me. Basically, I received the cold shoulder from the Augusta Chronicle. (Big surprise there!) Now it all makes sense. I can see why the Augusta Chronicle wanted the story to go away very quickly. If it lingered around too long, people would begin to wonder if the Augusta Chronicle was in collusion with Mr. Lewis.

Now is the time to admit my part in this whole fiasco. I should have just read this story, made a few comments, and kept on moving on. I feel bad about wasting my time and more importantly, other people's time on a publicity stunt. Every word in my open letter was sincere. I really do believe that an all-white basketball league would set the city of Augusta back a few decades. But at the same time, I feel foolish to even be associated with such a publicity stunt. So this essay is just a simple way for me to say, I've been had! The joke's on me and anyone else who got fired up over this issue. Looks like we got race hustled!!! Oh well, I guess you live and learn.

Note: I hope by the time this book goes to print, that the Augusta Chronicle will apologize to it's subscribers and readers for their inability to properly vet the press release of Don "Moose" Lewis.

A Tale of Two Cities— White/Black Augusta or Rich/Poor Augusta

Forty years ago on May 11, 1970, Augusta was a tale of two cities. You had a White Augusta, and a Black Augusta. The city was even as far as numbers (racial makeup), but that's where the similarities ended. There were both poor whites and poor blacks living in Augusta, but to be poor and black was a feeling that no poor white person could ever identify with. The reason being, had to do with disparities in just about every category imaginable. There certainly were disparities in just about every economic indicator, but the most devastating and lasting disparity had to do with basic human rights. Although the Jim Crow era had officially ended, Whites and Blacks were separate according to schools, neighborhoods, places of worship, and entertainment.

Has much really changed? If you look at it from a sole legal standpoint, then yes, things have drastically changed. Using the Charles Oatman Jr. situation as an example, there are no longer juveniles mixed in with adults in the penal system. Mental health is taken more seriously. There are more people of color on the police force. More people of color have been included in the lawmaking process. Augusta even elected a black mayor in the 80's. (Ed McIntyre) So I would be a fool if I said that nothing has changed.

However, there are still things that have remained the same. For instance, Augusta is still a tale of two cities. On the one hand, you have the Masters golf tournament, where the upper crust of society play. But if you were to venture straight down Washington Road into the inner city, you would see extreme cases of poverty. You have million-dollar homes in Westlake, which is in sharp contrast to the many trailer parks in Hephzibah. Instead of seeing a White and Black Augusta, would it be more accurate to actually see a Rich and Poor Augusta? Are there people and entities out there that have a vested interest in painting a picture of a racially divided Augusta, as opposed to an economically divided Augusta?

Unfortunately, certain organizations continue to miss the big picture as it relates to the haves and the have-nots. Instead, you have people squabbling over immigration reform, health care reform, and higher taxes. In just about every case, the interests of the rich and elite are interwoven and disguised as the interests of everyone. For years, this has been the biggest and most intricate shell game known to man. So the question remains, who profits the most from seeing people separating themselves physically, spiritually, mentally, and financially along racial lines? Keep your eyes, minds, and hearts open, and you may discover the answer. It's only cathartic when you come to this sobering conclusion on your own, rather than having someone tell you to answer. So keep watching!

(Part One) Black Youth of Augusta (America/World)— Are Adults Exploiting and Enabling our Kids?

For those of us not born or too young to remember what 1970 Augusta was like, it may seem like a long time ago. For those who lived through the turbulent Civil Rights movement and into the desegregation backlash of the 70s and 80s, 1970 Augusta may seem as if it was just yesterday. Whatever the case, you should be able to look at the events of the past and think about how far the CSRA has come.

There are both positives and negatives when it comes to the progression of our area, so let's start with the negatives first. In 40 years, we still see some of the same racial divisions in the city. Instead of these divisions being forced on people, many of them are by choice. As soon as you mention certain areas in Augusta, many people rightly make assumptions about the kind of people who live there. If I were to say Westlake, many people would envision huge and lavish homes. It just so happens that many of the inhabitants that live in Westlake are predominantly white. However, the neighborhood doesn't necessarily exclude by race, but rather by income. If I were to say Underwood Homes, Allen Homes, or Cherry Tree Crossing, most people would think about an all-black housing development. These areas also exclude by income. If I were to mention Josey, Glenn Hills, or Laney high school, most people would picture a predominately black high school. Unfortunately, many in the community would associate the excellence of athletics with the schools, rather than academics. That's certainly an image that needs to change! If I were to mention Lakeside or Greenbriar, many would picture a predominately white school. I am just using the areas of housing and schools to show how Augusta is still segregated, but not so much by race, but mainly by income. But why are the majority of the poor areas inhabited by blacks, and the majority of the well-to-do areas inhabited by whites?

That's really the million-dollar question, and you don't need a multimillion dollar government study to figure out the answer. From many in the black community, we hear the message of education resonating from every which way. Radio, TV, newspapers, all call for our black youth to rise up and meet the challenge of overcoming poverty by getting a good education. So what's the problem! Our youth are getting mixed messages from the black community, that's the major problem. You have intellectuals who call for economic empowerment and higher education, but then you have the entertainment world glamorizing sex, drugs, and violence. Are young people getting together and deciding to make raunchy music and distributing it en masse? Are young people the ones that are making these rap videos that exploit women? Do children put together millions of dollars in order to make movies that glamorize violence? Of course not!

It takes complicit adults, who have the power structure and organizational abilities, that enable them to globally distribute a negative message and image to our youth. Adults in thousand dollar three piece Armani suits are deciding what type of music makes it to your kids' eardrums. Sure, they may hire some young people from the street to scout talent, but you better believe that the mature adults have the final say. Adult program directors at radio stations are the ones who decide what music is played on your child's radio. Adult movie executives in Hollywood decide what movies your kids have the option of seeing. The same can be said for television. So my point is, why are there so many adults calling the young generation out on the carpet, when it is the adults who set such a hypocritical example? Why are the adults complaining about generation X and Y, when they are making money hand over fist off of these young people?

So when we see so many impoverished black youths in the CSRA embracing the negative lifestyles pushed at them, we as sensible adults know that it's all just a pipe dream. It doesn't even have to be a negative lifestyle, it could just be an overly flashy and impractical lifestyle. Everybody can't be a Lebron James or Drake, but if they study hard and apply themselves in school, they will have a high success rate in life. As a middle school teacher in the CSRA, I am thoroughly convinced that the number one threat to our black youth, is high expectations as far as money and a lavish lifestyle, but low expectations in the classroom. Thus far, I have not mentioned the responsibility of parents, because that's a whole other issue. My call to action is for the adults to realize as a whole, that they are setting the agenda for our young people. Do you want to exploit and enable, or steer kids in the right direction? If you choose to enable and exploit, please don't complain about the young people today, because then you would only be complaining about yourself.

(Part Two)—There is Hope! (Positives for our Area)

I promised positives in part one, so that's how I want to end this discussion. We can talk all day about how black people lag in every socioeconomic category known to man, but there are success stories that defy the statistics. Let's start off with the pride of our educational system here in Richmond County, Davidson. Davidson is racially and ethnically diverse, and is a perennial powerhouse in the United States when it comes to academic performance. In fact, many of our magnet schools are performing at high levels with a diverse student population. Every student that attends these schools has their priorities straight. If they lose focus, then they may find themselves elsewhere, losing out on a tremendous opportunity.

As far as housing, we are seeing newer neighborhoods pop up with more diversity. Is this because the economic gaps are closing, maybe. What about socially? The Arts in the Heart festival is a great event that promotes diversity and unity. You would be hard-pressed to find a more diverse crowd anywhere in this area. Not only that, but if you look around town, more ethnic restaurants are flourishing. (Indian, Pakistani, Italian, Asian, etc.) The Hispanic flavor of Augusta is starting to become more noticeable. All of these things add to the positives for our area. With the fusion of an array of different ethnicities and races, we can see more than a White and Black Augusta. Unfortunately, in this system of things you will probably always see a Poor and Rich Augusta. But the individual goal should be to move as many people out of the Poor Augusta into the Rich Augusta. The only way to realistically do that, is by stressing and promoting education in Poor Augusta.

May 11—Why should Augusta remember the 1970 Race Riot?

"You need to let that go!" "That was a long time ago!" "I don't want to get people riled up." "Stop playing the race card!" We have come so far and a lot of things have changed, so why do you want to bring up bad memories?" These are all trains of thought as to why the date of May 11, 1970 should be downplayed and very low-keyed. When it comes to race, people have a tendency to want to avoid candid, meaningful, and sometimes painful discussions, for fear of confrontation or animosity. I think that is what Atty. Gen. Eric Holder meant when he said: "When it comes to the issue of race, America is a nation of cowards." He took a lot of criticism for that comment, but dates like May 11, 2010, may prove Eric Holder to be exactly correct in his assessment.

In the opening paragraph, I gave you some reasons why many (both white and black people) in the CSRA may want to downplay the 40th year anniversary of the Augusta race riot. But here are some counter arguments that I have thought of: "Many people are new to the area, and may not know this part of Augusta's history." "Many kids and adults were not even born during the 70's, and may be interested in these events." "It is important to analyze the events and conditions that happened and existed before the riot, because maybe we can learn from them." "Some of the same conditions of poverty, hopelessness, and despair still exist in the black community today." "It would be beneficial to educate the community on what can happen if certain segments of the community are neglected." "It shows how a Black problem can quickly turn into a problem for the whole community." I could go on and on, but this old adage sums up the reasons for fully examining the events of the race riot: Those who forget the past, are doomed to repeat it.

So how can a discussion on the riot be driven, so as to benefit the community as a whole? For starters, the conditions that existed in Augusta as it relates to the inner-city, still exist today. If you were to walk through the streets of the Turpin Hill and surrounding communities, you will see lots of inadequate housing.

Also, many problems have developed that were not there in the1970s. (Drugs, teenage pregnancy, etc.) Add to all of this the abysmal educational gap and dropout rate of the inner-city youth, and you have many relevant issues to sink your teeth into. Using the riot as a reference point, you can ask the question: Why has there not been substantial progress in the inner-city? Is society, the government, parents, the inner-city itself, or all of the above to blame for ghetto stagnation. It is no coincidence that many of the Richmond County high schools up for federal grant money are predominantly black. The black community needs to ask the hard questions, as painful or self-incriminating as they may be, in order to develop some solutions to the problem. Simultaneously, the community as a whole, should be looking at black and inner-city problems as their own problems to. When black poverty and education is improved, it reflects on the area as a whole.

Another aspect of the race riot was the tensions between the police and the inner-city. Anyone that had lived through the riot could tell you that police/community relations have come a long way. Not only is there more diversity among the police, but people of color have risen in the ranks. Even though Augusta has had occasional controversies involving its police, for the most part cooler heads have prevailed.

The last issue that the riot sheds light on, is social interaction among various races. This may be one of the slowest areas of improvement. After all, you can't make people be around each other. As a rule of thumb, people tend to feel more comfortable around those people that they have the most in common with. Once again, I go back to education. Education combined with tolerance goes a long way. Let's be honest here for a minute, the Augusta race riot created a great deal of animosity, mistrust, and stagnation here in Augusta. When you add the still standing federal court order to desegregate schools, it's a miracle that the city has shown great progress. With that being said, the riot, while a painful reminder of the past, can be used to show the strength and promise of the city of Augusta. The lessons of the riot should not be lost on present and future generations. So let's all think of productive ways to recognize May 11, 2010.

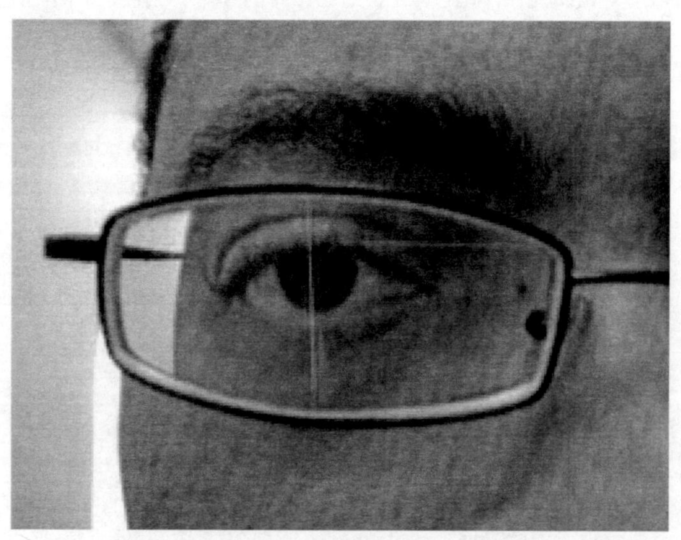

Can you see what I see?

Why do nice places of worship exist side by side in neighborhoods that look like this—(Turn Page)

Things that make you go HMMMMMMM!!!!
(shout out to Arsenio Hall)

ACKNOWLEDGMENTS

A very special thank you goes out to my mother, Marilyn Washington, who has continued to show tremendous faith in my judgment and ability. She still continues to be there for me through thick and thin.

- Thanks to Grady Abrams for imparting his knowledge and wisdom. In exile no more!!!
- Thanks to all those in the media who have supported my efforts: Tom Grant and Jill Peterson—My first T.V. Interview
- Ben Hasan—2nd T.V. interview—Always keeping the community informed!
- Helen Blocker Adams—First lady of Augusta Radio—Carl Thornton Jr.—Speaking with . . . Thanks for supporting me.
- Newspapers-Rachael Johnson-Aiken Standard-thanks for your interest. Metro Spirit—Stacy Eidson-Thanks for your support.
- Augusta State Bell Ringer—Pat Riley—Not the coach!
- Call and Post-Cleveland, OH-Rhonda and Jonathan
- Janice Jenkins and Kelby Walker—Always listening to Community Matters.
- All of the local news stations: WRDW/WJBF/WFXG/WAGT—Thanks Blayne A. for your great coverage on tough issues. Estelle and Jill (Behind the scenes) Thanks for giving Tutt Middle an experience of a lifetime. Jay Jefferies: Thanks to you and your family in Cleveland for sending me those copies of the Call and Post!
- Thanks to Brandi Cummings and WIS—She went to bat for me in Columbia S.C.
- On Point Crew-Cynthia, Laura, and That Teowanna! Keep Columbia informed.

- To all the National Media: Rob Redding Jr.—For giving me my first shot on his syndicated show.(Redding News Review)
- Mike McConnell-Cin. OH/ Rude Awakening-Ocean City, MD/ Mike and Jesse-Brownwood, TX (I may have to take you up on that Texas BBQ offer) Dave and The Morning Zone crew at KGAB in Wyoming
- Thanks Aunt Lillie for having that book signing for me! Thanks Henry, great cooking!!
- My son Jordan—hang in there!!!
- My brothers and sister—Tai-ri/Ronald and Aireka
- My family in Atlanta/Virgina—(Val, Cat, Jamiah(Doc), Calvin, Rose and all related family) Tracy and Family in AL. Lil Calvin and Philip.
- Grandma Naiomi and Mitch (Queens, N.Y.) Can't wait to visit again.
- Anthony Hawthorne—The Angry Black Man Model (Thanks for being a Good Sport!)
- Theophilus Moss—The Man with the Plan.
- Geoff Gregg-Missed you last time!
- Harry "Hippie" Hughes—No freebies!
- Carlton Holden—King of all Intellects!!
- Franklin Mars and Susie—You guys have been true friends. Thanks!!!
- Edward Maner—Thanks for inspiring me to write and your kind words of encouragement.

Last, but definitely not least, I would like to thank ***Jehovah*** for every positive blessing to ever come my way.

This is why we need to "Dig a Little Deeper":

*"**thinking ability** itself will **keep guard** over you, **discernment** itself will **safeguard you**, to **deliver** you from the bad way, from the man (*or woman*) speaking perverse things, from those leaving the paths of uprightness to walk in the ways of darkness, from those who are rejoicing in doing bad, who are joyful in the perverse things of badness;those whose paths are crooked and who are devious in their general course . . .*

New World Translation of the Holy Scriptures

Proverbs 2:11-15

I can't say it any better than that!

REFERENCES

Unless otherwise noted all source material came from the following websites:

- *www.wikipedia.com*
- **All books in the "Racial Book Review"**